THE
MORAVIAN GRAVEYARDS
OF
LITITZ, PA., 1744-1905

METALMARK BOOKS

The Moravian Graveyards of Lititz, Pa.,

1744-1905.

BY ABRAHAM REINKE BECK.

The Moravian Graveyards of Lititz, Pa.

The first, or "old," graveyard, a small tract a quarter of an acre or so in extent, is situated within the borough limit a short distance west of the junction of Broad and Centre Streets. On its eastern boundary, two hundred feet back from the king's highway, in the woods, stood the log church which had been built by George Klein (on his land), John Bender, Jacob Scherzer, Hartmann Verdriess, Lutherans, supported by a number of adherents of the Reformed and Mennonite denominations, for the Rev. Lawrence Nyberg, a Swedish Lutheran minister of Lancaster, who subsequently united with the Moravians. Consecrated on St. James' Day, July 25, 1744, it was thenceforth called the St. James' Church. In 1749 the majority of these worshipers, who had been spiritually awakened by the preaching in this vicinity of Count Zinzendorf, in 1742, organized the Warwick (Moravian) Country Congregation, and in 1759 they united with the Lititz congregation. With the completion of the new chapel (second story of the present parsonage,) in 1763, the use of the St. James' Church, except for occasional funeral services, was abandoned; but the graveyard continued to be the burial place of the Warwick members until 1791, when they began to bury in the new graveyard, although some of them were interred in the former plot as late as 1812. Later the remains of some few friendless persons, or vagrants, were buried there.

When, in 1889, the Trustees of that time, actuated by a praiseworthy motive, gave this old graveyard a complete renovation—eradicating a jungle of brambles, repairing the enclosure, and planting trees there—the tombstones, which had been taken up in leveling the ground, were relaid, in exact, straight rows, to be sure, but with such indiscriminate misplacement that their true individual sites are now hopelessly lost; fortunately, the erring stones are covered to a depth of some inches with vegetable mould and grass.

MEMBERS OF THE WARWICK CONGREGATION INTERRED ON THE FIRST, OR ST. JAMES' GRAVEYARD.

1744 to 1747.

1. Michael Beymüller's child.
2. Christian Weisskoph's child.
3. Gottlieb Veil's child. Two years old.
4. Anna Mary Henrich. Thirty-six years old.

1748.

5. Vincent Stauber. March 4. Fifty-five.
6. Mary Catharine Schmidt. March 25. Forty-seven.
7. Frederick Hayer.
8. Conrad Bassler. June 16.

1749.

9. Philip Plattenberger. April 11. Eight years old.
10. Verona Bender. Wife of John Bender. April 17. Forty-two years.
12. Michael Palmer. Sept. 20. Forty years.
13. John Philip Seip. Sept. 24. Eight months old.
14. Andrew Bort. Oct. 5. Fifty years.
15. Henry Possard. Oct. 9. Thirty years.
16. Jacob Johnson. Son of Jacob Johnson, Sr. Ten years old. Exercising himself in jumping, at the same time holding an open knife in his hand, he fell upon it, the blade piercing his heart, and death ensuing one minute later. Funeral service by Brother Ronner.

1750.

18. Elizabeth Palmer. Jan. 5. Thirty-eight.
20. Franciscus Seip. March 3. Eight years.
21. John George Kiesel. Infant son of Nicholas Kiesel.
22. Christian Huehter. Infant.
23. Carl Palmer. Infant.

1751.

24. Christina Johnson. Aug. 25. Infant daughter of Jacob and Juliana Johnson.
25. Jacob Palmer. Thirteen years old. Son of Michael Palmer. Funeral service by Brother Nixdorff.

1752.

27. Beatus Heil.
28. Frederick Bort. Three years old.

1753.

29. John Weidman. Infant son of John Henry Weidman.
30. John Sherzer. Son of Stephen Sherzer. Two years.
31. John Michael Eib. Nov. 5. Thirty years. Three children: Margaret Barbara, Michael and Jacob.

32. **Elizabeth Bechtel.** Widow. Aged seventy-seven years. Funeral service by Brother Christian Henry Rauch.
33. **Anna Mary Seip.** Infant.

1754.

34. **Andrew Koerber.** Seven days old. Baptized by the mid-wife.
35. **Andrew Frey.** Son of Christopher Frey. Two years. Funeral service by Brother Bader.

1755.

36. **Anna Maria Bassler.** Widow. Fifty-two.
37. **Anna Maria Kiesel.** Wife of Frederick Kiesel. Thirty-four. Funeral service by Brother Krogstrup.
38. **Peter Heil.** Infant son of Jacob Heil.
39. **Michael Eib.** Son of John Michael Eib. Five years.

1756.

40. **Susanna Frey.** Wife of Andrew Frey. Mother of Christopher Frey. Sixty years. Funeral service by Brother Lembke.
41. **Christian Ludwig Lembke.** Son of the Rev. Franz Christian Lembke. Born in Nazareth, July 20, 1755. Six months. Funeral service by Brother Russmeyer.
42. **Juliana Margaretha Johnson.** Wife of Jacob Johnson. Forty-two.
43. **John Michael Blickensderfer.** Infant son of Christian and Catharina Blickensderfer.
44. **Catharine Weidman.** Wife of Henry Weidman. Twenty-two.
45. **Andrew Frey.** Sept. 16. Sixty-five.

1757.

46. **Thomas Williams.** March 4. Fifty years. Funeral service by Brother Neisser.
47. **Catharine Bender.** Infant daughter of John Bender. One year.
48. **John William Boehler.** Aged five years. Died of small-pox.
49. **Carl Frederick Palmer.** Ten months.
50. **George Blickensderfer.** ⎫ Twin sons of Christian and Catharine
51. **Daniel Blickensderfer.** ⎬ Blickensderfer. Infants.
52. **Infant son of Nicholas Jungblut.**
53. **John Michael Seip.** One year.
54. **Anna Ramsberg.** Born in Norway, Jan. 26, 1706; died in Lititz, Oct. 28. She was the General Superintendent of the Single Sisters in the Pennsylvania Country Congregations.

1758.

55. **John Frederick Ricksecker.** Son of Peter Ricksecker. Eight months.
56. **Barbara Plattenberger.** Wife of John Plattenberger. Forty-six.
57. **Samuel Frey.** Infant son of Christopher Frey.
58. **Anna Rosina Plattenberger.** Infant daughter of John Plattenberger.
59. **Anna Rosina Kling.** Infant daughter of Christian Kling.
60. **John George Lecron.** Died Aug 3. Aged nine years.

63. **Louise Leçon.** Died Aug. 9. Wife of Paul Leçon. Sixty-five years of age.

64. **John Daniel Lecron.** Died Aug. 10. Aged twelve years. Oldest son of Daniel and Mary (Thomas) Lecron. As he and his brother, John George, were pupils of Brother Russmeyer, in the "Warwick School-house," the latter having been one of his brightest boys, they have been included here, although they were buried on their father's farm.

65. **Christina Kiesel.** Infant daughter of Nicholas Kiesel.

66. **Matthew Baumgaertner.** Infant.

67. **Thomas Jungblut.** Infant.

68. **Benigna Kiesel.** Infant.

69. **David Bieler.** Eight years.

70. **Michael Hilton.** Infant son of David Hilton.

71. **Catharine Jungblut.** Three years.

72. **John Haller.** Son of Henry Haller. Seven years.

73. **Elizabeth Broksch,** m.n. Helwig. Born Feb. 24, 1700. Wife of the Rev. Andrew Broksch, pastor of the Warwick congregation. Funeral service by Brother Russmeyer. The Single Sisters paid for her grave-stone.

74. **John Christian Kling.** Born in the city of Worms, Jan. 14, 1705. Died Nov. 7, 1758.

75. **John Frey.** Infant.

1759.

76. **Anna Maria Blickensderfer.** Infant.

1760.

77. **Paul Tshudy.** Born in Donegal, Pa., 1754. Son of Nicholas Tshudy. Aged six years.

78. **John Michael Heil.** Aged two years. Drowned in the Lititz creek on his father's farm adjoining the Lititz tract on the east.

78. **Christina Veit.** Born in Pfaffenhofen, Würtemberg, 1714.

80. **Beata Struebig.**

81. **Elizabeth Westhaeffer.** Infant.

1762.

82. **John George Kiesel.** Born in Igelheim, Palatinate, 1680.

1763.

83. **Franz Seip.** Aged forty-eight years.

84. **Eva Barbara Tshudy.** Infant daughter of Nicholas Tshudy.

1764.

85. **Andrew Palmer.** Infant.

86. **Christian Kling.** Son of John Christian Kling. Met his death in falling from a tree. Thirteen years.

87. **A still-born infant** of Peter and Anna Maria Huber.

88. **Matthew Ricksecker.** Infant son of Peter Ricksecker.

1766.

89. **Paul Leçon.** Born in Lausanne, May, 1686. He was one of the Huguenot refugees. His daughter, Catharine, married Nicholas Tshudy. His wife and he were of the first members of the Warwick congregation in 1749. The name was usually written "Lesson." Died Oct. 13, aged eighty years.

90. **John Hilton.** Infant son of David Hilton.

91. **Anna Maria Frey.** Daughter of Christoph Frey. Aged five years.

1769.

92. **Anna Maria Kiesel.** March 27. Daughter of Frederick and Verona Kiesel. Aged twelve years.

93. **Frederick Kiesel.** April 13. Same parents. Died of small-pox, aged six years.

94. **Nathaniel Kiesel.** April 23. Same parents. Small-pox. Aged four years.

95. **Verona Kiesel.** April 30. Sister of the foregoing. Small-pox. Aged eleven years.

96. **Daniel Lecron.** May 3. Born in the Palatinate, near Heidelberg, in 1712. Came to this country in 1741. Lived first in Lancaster and then moved to Warwick. His second wife was a sister of John Thomas, baker, of Lititz. Deeply impressed by hearing his children pray the religious verses they had learned of Brother Russmeyer, in the Warwick school, he was led to unite with the Brethren, first, in 1759, as an associate, and finally in 1765 as a full member of the Lititz congregation. Funeral service by Brother Grubé. He was of Huguenot origin.

97. **Samuel Struebig.** Aged one year. Died of small-pox.

98. **Eberhard Palmer.** A son of Christian and Barbara Palmer. Died of small-pox, aged eleven years.

99. **Susanna Gutjahr.** Infant daughter of John Christian and Margaret Gutjahr.

1770.

100. **Barbara Ricksecker,** m.n. Bechtel. Born 1717 in Bahnbruecken, near Heilbronn. Thrice married; her first husband was Henry Klein, her second, Andrew Bort, and her third, Peter Ricksecker. Died Jan. 27, aged fifty-two years.

101. **Joseph Westhaeffer.** Infant son of George Michael Westhaeffer.

102. **John Christian Grosh.** John Grosh's son, aged three years.

1771.

103. **Maria Margaretha Ricksecker,** m.n. Thomas. Born April 4, 1723, in Pfullingen, Würtemberg. The widow of Daniel Lecron, she was married in 1770 to Peter Ricksecker. Died April 10, aged forty-eight years.

104. **John Philip Sherzer.** Infant son of the associate member Jacob Sherzer, a resident of Manheim.

105. **Gottfried Grosh.** Infant son of John Grosh.

1772.

106. **Elizabeth Heil.** Daughter of Jacob and Anna Catharine Heil.
Aged twenty-two years. December 6.

107. **Anna Catharine Heil,** born Ruehl. Born in Schoharie, N. Y., June
5, 1715 Wife of Jacob Heil. They united with the Brethren in 1749.
Had sixteen children. Their farm adjoined the Lititz tract on the
east. Died Dec. 23, aged fifty-eight years. Funeral service on
Christmas Day by Bishop Hehl.

1773.

108. **Christina Margaretha Kiesel,** m.n. Stein. Born on Christmas
Day, 1684, in Boeht, near Speier. Married John George Kiesel in
1712, and in 1762 they celebrated their Golden Wedding. Of her
seven children she was survived by her sons Nicholas and Frederick. She and her husband were spiritually awakened in 1743 by
the preaching of the Brethren, who, before either the St. James'
church or the Warwick *Gemeinhaus* were built, frequently held
service in their house; and in 1749 they united with the congregation. As a faithful and experienced *wehmutter* she assisted at the
birth of three hundred children. Died Dec. 3, aged eighty-nine
years.

109. **Christina Westhaeffer,** m.n. Sandritter. Born in the Palatinate,
June 21, 1713. In 1732 she came to this country, and in the same
year was married to Valentine Westhaeffer. They united with the
Brethren at Muddy Creek (Reamstown) in 1746. Moravian ministers, traveling from Bethlehem to Lititz, found their home a
pleasant resting-place and Sister Westhaeffer always a generous
hostess. She died Dec. 6, aged sixty years.

1774.

110. **John Christian Huber.** Son of Peter and Anna Maria Huber. Died
July 26, aged six years.

1775.

111. **John Ludwig Westhaeffer.** A son of Conrad and Catharine Westhaeffer. Aged six years.

112. **Daniel Westhaeffer.** Infant son of George Michael Westhaeffer.
Died May 4.

113. **George Michael Westhaeffer, Jr.** Died May 4, aged twelve years.
Small-pox.

1776.

114. **John Henry Frey.** A son of Christian and Regina Frey; aged two
years.

115. **Maria Margaret Grosh.** A daughter of Philip Grosh. Died of
small-pox, aged six years.

116. **Elizabeth Risksecker.** A daughter of Jacob Ricksecker. Died of
small-pox, aged two years.

117. **John Frderick Ricksecker.** A son of Jacob Ricksecker. Died of
small-pox, aged eight months.

1777.

118. **John Kiesel.** Son of Frederick Kiesel. Small-pox. Aged nine
years.
119. **Maria Margaret Cassler.** A daughter of Catharine Cassler, late
Bort. Aged two years.
120. **Anna Christina Ricksecker.** Unmarried Sister. Born in the
Earldom of Leiningen-Wüsterburg, May 3, 1734. Came as an
orphan to this country with her uncle, Peter Ricksecker, by whom
she was brought up. Died May 28, aged forty-three years.
121. **John Gutjahr.** Infant son of Gottfried Gutjahr.

1778.

122. **Jacob Blickensderfer.** He was born in the Palatinate, Feb. 13,
1752. Came with his parents, Christian and Catharina (Sherger)
Blickensderfer, in his second year, to this country. Lived here
until 1766, when he moved to York where he married Elizabeth
Ilgenfritz. A year before his death he returned to this neighborhood. Died Jan. 20, of the then epidemic "camp-fever," aged
twenty-six years.
123. **Peter Ricksecker.** Born in the Canton of Berne, Switzerland, Oct.
20, 1710. Came to this country in his thirtieth year. In 1743 he
married the widow Anna Jung, in Donegal, Pa., and there they
were of the first members of that Moravian congregation. They
had three sons, Jacob, Peter, and John. His second wife was the
widow Bort, and with her he moved from Donegal to the Bort
farm in this neighborhood and united with this congregation. Of
his six children by this marriage he was survived by Christian,
Gertrude, Anna Johanna, and Elizabeth. His third and fourth
wives were the widows Margaretha Lecron and Anna Schneider.
For many years he was the Steward of the congregation and
Superintendent of the children. Died Feb. 9, aged sixty-seven
years.
124. **Christian Palmer.** Born in August, 1703, near Sinsheim, in the
Palatinate. Came to this country in 1733, and married the widow
Susanna Brunck, with whom he had six children. His second
wife, to whom he was married by Pastor Nyberg, was the widow
Barbara Pichler; they had seven children. He died March 8,
aged seventy-four years.
125. **Michael Grosh.** Infant son of Philip Grosh.

1780.

126. **Joseph Gutjahr.** Infant son of Joseph Gutjahr.

1781.

127. **Catharine Shoenlein.** Infant daughter of Leonhard Shoenlein.
128. **Anna Apollonia Sherzer,** m.n. Glockenberger. Born Dec. 14, 1711,
in the Palatinate. Came to this country with her husband, Jacob
Sherzer, in 1738. They were of the first members of the War-

wick congregation. She had five children; Jacob, Philip, and Leonhard surviving her. Died July 16, aged forty-five years.

129. **Barbara Grosh,** m.n. Bort. Born July 20, 1741. Wife of John Grosh. Died Dec. 10, of consumption, aged forty years.

130. **Barbara Margaret Shoenlein.** Infant daughter of Leonhard Shoenlein.

131. **John Bender.** Born in Kirchardt, Baden, September, 1701. Came to this country in 1741. United with the Brethren in 1760. Died April 10, aged eighty-one years. Nine children.

132. **John Frederick Ricksecker.** Infant son of Jacob Ricksecker.

133. **Maria Barbara Ricksecker.** Infant daughter of John Ricksecker.

1783.

134. **Anna Margaret Bender.** Born Sept. 27, 1711, in the Palatinate. Second wife of John Bender. She had one child, a son, who survived her.

135. **Jacob Heil.** Born in Rohrbach, Palatinate, April 1712. Came to this country in 1730. Married Catharina Ruehl, both uniting with the Warwick Brethren in 1749. Nine of his sixteen children survived him. Died Sept. 5, aged seventy-two years.

136. **Christian Henry Westhaeffer.** Infant son of Conrad Westhaeffer.

1784.

137. **Barbara Kiesel,** m.n. Boehler. Born in 1716. Wife of John Nicholas Kiesel. Died Sept. 17, aged sixty-eight years.

138. **Joseph Shober.** Infant son of Andrew Shober.

1785.

139. **Christoph Frey.** Born May 19, 1721, in Hornbach, Rhenish Bavaria. Came with his parents, Andrew and Susanna Frey, to this country in 1733. Married Margaret Beyer. United with the Warwick Brethren in 1749. Of his eleven children, two sons and four daughters survived him. Died July 30, aged sixty-five years. Funeral service by Bishop Ettwein.

140. **Valentine Westhaeffer.** Born Jan. 1, 1703, in the village of Hohen-Sachsen, between Weinheim and Heidelberg. In 1731 he embarked for America and, after a dreadful voyage of six months duration during which his wife and child and most of the emigrant passengers perished from hunger or thirst, or other maladies, landed in Philadelphia, where, after a few years, he married Christina Sandritter. They had five children; two married sons survived him. He and his wife after being spiritually awakened by the brethren in Oley, united with them at Muddy Creek, in 1746, and were of the first members of that congregation; after its abandonment they belonged to the Warwick congregation. He resided in Lititz 1764-'65, and after his wife's death lived with his sons. Died of dropsy May 12, aged eighty-three years. Funeral service by Brother Dencke.

141. **John Koch.** Born in September, 1705, in Alsace. Converted in Lancaster by the preaching of Zinzendorf. He was one of those members of the Rev. Lawrence Nyberg's congregation who, with their pastor, came over to the Brethren. By trade a wheelwright. He died on his son-in-law John Hoefer's place, five miles from Lititz, July 31, aged eighty-two years.

142. **Nicholas Jungblut.** Born in 1712 in Bechingen, near Landau, Palatinate. His first wife and three children died at sea. In 1743 he married Anna Maria Kappler. Because of a hostile incursion of Indians they were forced to flee hither from their home in Bethel on the Swatara, and here they remained permanently. Ten children. He died Dec. 30, on his place "above the large spring," aged seventy-five years.

1788.

143. **Anna Margaretha Frey,** m.n. Bayer. Born in 1727 in Rhenish Bavaria. Wife of Christoph Frey. Died Sept. 4.

144. **Benjamin Hoefer.** Infant.

145. **Elizabeth Kreiter.** Infant daughter of Michael Christian Kreiter.

1791.

146. **Elizabeth Westhaeffer,** m.n. Kling. Born in Chester County, in 1733; a daughter of Christian and Eva Maria Kling. Died Jan. 18. Wife of George Michael Westhaeffer.

147. **John Christian Gutjahr.** Born Oct. 15, 1714, in Werseburg, Saxony. Married, in Lancaster, 1746, Margaretha Roesner. Nine of his twelve children survived him. Farmer and hatter. Died on his place near Lititz, Feb. 12, aged seventy-six years. One of his descendants was Charles Goodyear, the discoverer of the process for the vulcanization of rubber.

148. **John Nicholas Kiesel.** Born Sept. 24, 1716, in Igelsheim, Palatinate. A son of John George and Christine Margaret (Stein) Kiesel. Married Barbara Boehler. Of twelve children, six survived him. Died Nov. 3, aged seventy-five years.

1792.

149. **Anna Maria Jungblut,** m.n. Kappler. Born Oct. 6, 1718, in Kirchardt, Baden. Wife of Nicholas Jungblut. Died July 28, aged seventy-four years.

1793.

150. **Christian Frey.** Born in Hempfield Township, 1748; a son of Christoph Frey. Farmer. Died March 4, aged forty-five years.

1794.

151. **Jacob Sherzer.** Born Aug. 3, 1712, in Michelfelde, Palatinate. Came with his wife Anna Apollonia (Glockenberger) to this country in 1738. Died on his place, near Lititz, Jan. 19, aged eighty-one years.

152. **Anna Maria Huber,** late Eib. Born at sea, Aug. 10, 1727. Her parents were George and Eva (Hammer) Schwab, from the Palat-

inate. They settled in Earl Township. By her first marriage to Michael Eib she had three children; and nine by her second marriage to Peter Huber. Died Jan. 26, aged sixty-six years.

1795.

153. **Philip Koch.** Unmarried. Born in Kussel, Rhenish Bavaria, in 1730. A weaver in the Brethren's House. Died Dec. 6, aged sixty-five years.

1798.

154. **Rebecca McClelland.** Infant daughter of Peter McClelland.
155. **George Huber.** Oldest son of Peter and Rosina (Gutjahr) Huber. Aged seventeen years.
156. **Peter Huber, Sr.** Born July 15, 1735, in Berlin. Came to this country in 1741. His first wife was Anna Maria Schwab; his second, the Widow Martin (born Sherzer). Died Aug. 1, aged sixty-three years.
157. **Anna Regina Frey.** Born in 1755; a daughter of Peter Huber, and wife of Christian Frey. Died Aug. 10, aged forty-two years.
158. **John Huber.** Born in 1765. Having come to Lititz to settle the estate of his father, Peter Huber, he died Sept. 22, aged thirty-three years.

1799.

159. **Eva Maria Kling,** m.n. Zimmer. Born in 1724, in Germany. Wife of Christian Kling. Died April 14, aged seventy-six years.
160. **Matthew McClelland.** Infant son of Peter McClelland, a Presbyterian neighbor.
161. **Magdalena Werner.** Infant daughter of Matthew Werner.

1800.

162. **Zacharias Heil.** Born in 1738; a son of Jacob Heil. Aged sixty-two years.

1801.

163. **Elizabeth Bernthaeusel.** Child of Michael Bernthaeusel.
164. **Joseph Glancy Stoehr.** Child of John Stoehr.

1802.

165. **Catharina Barbara Grosh.** Infant daughter of John Grosh.
166. **Andrew Noble.** A drover, living fifteen miles above Carlisle, who had come hither with a herd of cattle, was taken sick, could go no farther, and died in the Lititz tavern.
167. **Evans.** Stillborn child of James and Margaretha Evans.

1804.

168. **Elizabeth Rock.** Child of George Rock, shoemaker.
169. **Hannah Grosh.** A daughter of Jacob Grosh, of Hempfield Township. Aged three years.

1805.

170. **Elizabeth Bernthaeusel.** Child of Michael Bernthaeusel, saddler.
171. **Henry Werner.** Infant son of Matthew Werner, day-laborer.

1806.

172. **Catharine Rickert.** Infant daughter of Daniel and Magdalena (Goepfert) Rickert.
173. **Elizabeth Fuhrman,** m.n. Rock. Born Aug. 1, 1765, in Cocalico Township. Wife of Conrad Fuhrman. Died July 4, aged forty years.
174. **James Evans.** Born in 1761, in Ireland. Aged forty-four years. Died April 23. He was an ancestor of the Lititz Evans family. By occupation a day-laborer.

1807.

175. **Daniel Rickert.** Child of Daniel Rickert.

1809.

176. **Ephraim Kiesel.** Aged three years. A son of Abraham Frederick Kiesel.
177. **Catharina Bernthaeusel,** m.n. Rock. Born July 26, 1770, in Cocalico Township. Wife of Michael Bernthaeusel. Died Feb. 19, aged forty years. Five sons and two daughters survived her.

1811.

178. **John Knox.** Born in Donaghkiddie, between Londonderry and Strabane, Ireland. For a number of years he was a farm-hand with Christian Blickensderfer, Sr., and later with John Muecke, near Lititz.

1812.

179. **George Diehm.** Child of Henry and Elizabeth (Geitner) Diehm.
180. **Salome Krall.** Daughter of Abraham Krall. Aged twenty years.
181. **Jacob Huber.** Died July 4.

THE SECOND GRAVEYARD.

The second, present, graveyard is situated on a gentle acclivity to the south of the church. It was laid out after the invariable manner of Moravian burial places—the tombstones to lie flat on the graves, the sexes in segregation—on the seventh of November, 1758; and we may safely conjecture that the existent venerable cedars bordering the first avenue were planted at about the same time.

The sections to the right (men and boys), and those to the left (women and girls), formed its original extent. Two additional sections increased its size in 1851. Its first enclosure — a low wall of loose stones — was removed in the second decade of the past century, and in its place was then erected a neat fence of pales having a noble entrance gate—its arched top on the side of approach appealing to religious sentiment with these words upon it in finely executed German text :

"𝕾𝖊𝖑𝖎𝖌 𝖘𝖎𝖓𝖉 𝖉𝖎𝖊 𝕿𝖔𝖉𝖙𝖊𝖓 𝖉𝖎𝖊 𝖎𝖓 𝖉𝖊𝖒 𝕳𝖊𝖗𝖗𝖓 𝖘𝖙𝖊𝖗𝖇𝖊𝖓."

and on the reverse, "I am the Resurrection and the Life." Great the pity that this gate was removed, about the year 1850, without any attempt to restore and retain its beautifully appropriate inscriptions.

The first Easter morning service in point of time was held on the St. James' graveyard on April 14, 1759, and concluded on the new graveyard with the Te Deum; and this order was continued until 1763 when the litany was read for the first time on the present graveyard, and repeated in the St. James' Church at 9 o'clock before the sermon. "April 3, 1763 : Early at 4 o'clock the congregation was awakened by the French-horns. As we left the chapel, in procession, for the graveyard, the '*waldhornisten*' played '*Allein Gott in der Höh' sey Ehr'.*' It snowed and rained hard."—Congregation Diary.

In 1770 trombones were substituted for the French-horns in the church-music.

At the sunrise service of Easter, March 26, 1780, the brightness of the lovely morning was suddenly eclipsed by the passing overhead of countless multitudes of wild pigeons flying, with their wonted swiftness, from North to South.

The first gravediggers for the second graveyard were the Brethren Heil and Baumgaertner.

The total number of those here interred down to April 1, 1905, is 1219.

EXPLANATION OF THE METHOD TO BE USED IN SEEKING THE LOCATION OF A GRAVE.

The avenues are numbered 1, 2, and 3; the rows of graves are given in Roman numerals, counting from the entrance to the graveyard—those to the right of each avenue being indicated by the letter r, and those to the left by the letter l; while the final numeral shows the local number of a grave, thus: Renatus-Keller, 1, r. xii, 6, February 22, means that Renatus Keller's grave is on Avenue 1, right side, twelfth row, and its local number is 6; and that he died on February 22. See draft annexed.

1758.

1. **John Baumgaertner.** 1, r. xiv, 1. Nov. 6. A son of Matthew and Barbara Baumgaertner, born in Lititz, Sept. 26. On November 8, the congregation assembled in front of the *Gemeinhaus* where the little corpse was exposed to view; and then, after an address by Bishop Hehl, in which he said that they would begin their new graveyard *"mit diesem ersten Saamen Körngen,"* the funeral procession "of more than eighty people," proceeded to the place of interment. There the usual burial litany was read; then, all kneeling, Bishop Hehl, in fervent prayer, consecrated the spot "for those who in the future should be buried there to rest in hope till that important moment when Christ shall call His own from their graves to a glorious resurrection."

1759.

2. **Peter Jacob Jürgensen.** 1, r. xi, 1. Sept. 4. Unmarried.

1760.

3. **Elizabeth Cassler.** 1, l. xiv, 1. April 19. Infant daughter of Lewis Cassler.

4. **Catharine Werner.** 1, l. xiv, 2. Sept. 10. Born April 2, 1759.

5. **Christian Frederick Steinman,** 1, r. xix, 7. Dec. 12. Born in Dresden, Saxony, Nov. 11, 1711. He married Anna Regina Rose, and emigrated with her to America, on the "Irene," in 1749. They arrived in Lititz, from Bethlehem, in 1756, and were to board the men at work on the congregation mill. His widow moved with her son, John Frederick, to Lancaster, where she (Widow Hayne) died, May 30, 1783. There are Moravian descendants of Christian Frederick Steinman living in that city; one of whom is George Steinman, the president of the Lancaster County Historical Society.

1762.

6. **Gottlieb Bezold.** 1, r. x, 1. Apr. 1. Unmarried. Born Nov. 1, 1720, at Bischofswerda, Saxony, where he lived as a young man, his trade that of pursemaker. Came to America, 1742, with the first "Sea Congregation." Ordained a Deacon in 1748. He was the Elder-General of all the unmarried men, ("Single Brethren") belonging to the American Moravian Church. Died while on a visit to Lititz, whither he had come to install Bro. Lorenz Bagge as the *Pfleger* (Spiritual Overseer) of the Single Brethren. Was the architect of the Lititz Brethren's House.

7. **Anna Rebecca Merck.** 1, l. xiv, 3. Aug. 24. Infant daughter of Henry and Rebecca Merck.

1764.

8. **Martin Bort.** 1, r. xi, 2. Oct. 23. Unmarried. Born in Warwick Township, Aug. 14, 1743. Learned shoemaking with Bro. Lewis Cassler.

1765.

9. **Abraham Haller.** 1, r. xi, 3. Oct. 11. Unmarried. Only son of John Henry and Anna Maria Haller. Born at Muddy Creek (Reamstown) Jan. 9, 1744.

10. **Anna Johanna Thomas.** 1, l. xiv, 4. Dec. 10. Infant of John and Maria Salome Thomas.

1767.

11. **John Christian Fenstermacher.** 1, r. xix, 6. Dec. 8. Born April 14, 1697, in Meissenheim, Rhenish Bavaria. After his apprenticeship he was for six years Court Butcher to the Count von Daun, on the Rhine, and then served one year in the Dutch war. In 1741 he came to Pennsylvania with his family. His wife died at sea, leaving him with three children, one of whom was the mother of Wm. Werner of Lititz. Arrived in Philadelphia, mentally, physically and financially depressed, he was soon comforted by Count Zinzendorf and others of the Brethren, whom he joined in 1748. May, 1749, he married the widow Barbara Leibert. Came to Lititz Sept. 1, 1764, to take charge of the congregation store, on his own account for a few years, when it was to be returned to the church. After a short illness of three days duration, he died, "a happy child of grace," aged seventy years.

1768.

12. **Anna Regina Niecke.** 1, l. xi, 1. March 10. Unmarried. Born in Reingenheim, near Manheim, April 22, 1737. In faithful service, seven years, with Fenstermacher's, and later at Bro. Jasper Payne's.

1769.

13. **Christina Baumgaertner.** 1, l. xiv, 5. March 23. Born Feb. 16, 1760. Daughter of Matthew Baumgaertner.

14. **Christina Cassler.** 1, l. xiv, 6. April 18. Third daughter of Lewis and Christina Cassler, born 1765. Died of small-pox.

15. **Anna Elizabeth Cassler.** i, l, xiv, 7. April 27. Same parents. Born July 6, 1767. Died of small-pox.
16. **Anna Maria Werner,** m.n. Schuchard. i, l. xix, 1. May 13. Born in Heidelberg Township, June 26, 1727. Married William Werner. They had five children; Catharina, and, surviving her, Rosina, Frederick, Nathaniel and John.

1770.

17. **Christian Henry Sproge.** i, r. xi, 4. May 16. Unmarried. Born April 23, 1729, in Curland near Bauske. By trade a mason. Came to Lititz, 1758, one of the original six brethren to occupy the new Brethren's House. Highly esteemed as superintendent of the larger boys. Some of his last work was the building of the first corpse depository (*Leichen Capellchen*), a vault in the basement of the *Gemeinhaus* (now the parsonage), and his own mortal remains were the first to lie there. (The entrance to this vault was on the west side of the house, under an outside stairway used by the brethren in going to the *Saal,* or meeting-place of the congregation, on the second floor. The present corpse-house was built, with the church, in 1787.)

1771.

18. **John Valentine Grosh.** i, r. xix, 5. April 17. Born Jan. 6, 1706, at Eichloch in the Palatinate. In 1728 he married Barbara Sandman. They had twelve children. In 1743 they came to Pennsylvania with five children remaining to them, and settled near Lititz. In 1749 he joined the Warwick (Moravian) Congregation, was its first chief-sacristan, and for many years its Steward. In 1764 he moved to Lititz, where he was appointed Curator of the Sisters' "Choir," and, again, chief sacristan. On April 15, of the above year, he was stricken with paralysis, remaining unconscious until his death. There are descendants of his living in Lititz.
19. **Carl August Ludewig.** i, r. xi, 5. July 2. Unmarried. Born March 9, 1729, in Wernerode, Thuringia. A potter.
20. **Gottlieb Coelln.** i, r. xiv, 2. July 7. Infant son of Claus and Elizabeth Coelln, and twin brother of John Coelln.
21. **Maria Barbara Geitner.** i, l. xiii, 1. Aug. 22. Born June 13, 1764. Daughter of John George Geitner.
22. **Christian Gottlieb Hoffman.** i, r. x, 2. Aug. 25. Unmarried. Born in Friedersdorf, Upper Lusatia, Dec. 21, 1715. For seven years, from 1765, he was the universally beloved *Pfleger* of the Single Brethren.
23. **Elizabeth Hall,** m.n. Kalkloeser. i, l. xix, 2. Oct. 3. Born in Germantown, Feb. 1, 1738. Married James Hall, Oct. 23, 1770. Died of complications arising from the birth of a son.
24. **Thomas Utley.** i, r. xi, 6. Nov. 11. An unmarried son of the Rev. Richard Utley, born in Bethlehem, June 27, 1751. Shoemaker. A consumptive, he came here in August, 1770, at the suggestion of Bro. Tobias Beckel, who was much attached to him, to have medical

treatment from a certain Dr. Blank—"the old Swiss doctor"—who at that time practised in this neighborhood. In connection with the burial of this Brother, the Brethren's House Diary gives us the following singular circumstance: When the gravedigger had partly filled in the grave he heard three distinct knocks which seemed to him to come from the inside of the coffin-lid. He quickly called a number of the brethren to the spot, and they decided to re-open the coffin, for if they failed to do so, an unfounded "talk" would be the result: therefore, it was taken up and opened; but Brother Thomas lay just as he had been deposited there, and not a sign of vitality was apparent. The brethren inferred that the knockings, which were heard again as they re-filled the grave, arose from the pressure of ground on the coffin-lid.

1772.

25. **Elizabeth Brinkman.** 1, l. xi, 2. March 8. Unmarried Sister. Born in York, Jan. 8, 1751.
26. **Abraham Delker.** 1, r. xi, 7. March 13. Unmarried. Born in Dornhan, Würtemberg, Aug. 26, 1746.
27. **Anna Hanke.** 1, l. xi, 3. May 19. Unmarried Sister. Born in Gnadenthal, near Nazareth, Feb. 6, 1748.
28. **Samuel Scheffel.** 1, r. xiv, 3. Nov. 21. Son of Ernst and Catharine Scheffel, born in Lititz, Nov. 9, 1770. Aged two years.

1774.

29. **Catharine Elizabeth Scheffel.** 1, l. xiii, 2. Feb. 20. Infant daughter of the foregoing parents.
30. **Christian Tshudy.** 1, r. xix, 4. March 3. Born in Warwick Township, April 20, 1741. His parents were Henry and Catharine Tshudy, members of the Warwick Moravian congregation. Married, 1762, Eva Barbara Kiesel. Moved to Lititz, 1762, hearty permission having been accorded him as "a worthy acquisition" to the community. Built a house on Main St., about midway of the present Seminary grounds, and followed his work as a day-laborer. He had four children: John Jacob, Christian, Anna Maria (married Rev. John Maehr) and Matthias. Christian Tshudy, Jr., moved to Ohio, where his descendants are living.
31. **Maria Christina Schmidt.** 1, l. xi, 4. April 19. The remarkable experience of this unmarried Sister deserves the larger space devoted to it. She was born in Conewago, near York, Pa., Aug. 1, 1746. At an early age the preaching of Moravian itinerants made an impression upon her heart, and she beseeched the Lord to make her His happy child and grant her wish to join, eventually, the sweet Sisterhood in Bethlehem. When the congregation at Manocasy (Graceham) Md., was founded, her father, Caspar Schmidt, and his family moved thither so that they might be with the Brethren. During the French and Indian War, when Christina was nine years old, in August, 1755, the dwellers in that locality were thrown into consternation by the swift irruption of a band of ravaging, murderous Indians (French). The Schmidts and others sought refuge

in the Moravian school-house, but Christina and her father were eight miles away from it on his plantation. Suddenly, from the forest, they heard the sharp crack of a rifle! The father threw his child upon a horse, telling her to ride as fast as she could to the shelter of the school-house, but the horse balked and refused to move, while several Indians appeared, rapidly crossing the clearing. Schmidt's first impulse was to remain with his daughter, but to do that he knew was to be killed on the spot, and others needed his protection; so he fled precipitately, fortunately escaping some bullets sent after him. Capturing Christina, an Indian swung her on to his back and made away with her, she vigorously protesting and making frantic appeal to be set free; to all of which he only answered "Yes, yes," and strode away the faster. In a desperation almost as comical as it was futile, she drew from her clothing *a pin* and with all her little force jabbed it into his broad back, which caused him to put her to the ground and despoil her of her pins. After that, a threatening tomahawk always kept her quiet. Now the whole band turned upon its homeward route, traveling northward. On this journey Christina's tender eyes beheld the most frightful massacres; and when, upon coming to one of their settlements destroyed by the English, the avenging Indians took some of her fellow-captives, bound them to trees, and, thrusting into their bodies pointed sticks of resinous wood, set fire to them—a continuant torture from morning to night—the savage fiends compelled her *to laugh with them* at the agony of their victims. Approaching their town—its score of dogs giving timely notice of their coming—they were met and welcomed with wild shouting and much rude drumming, by the young braves and the women and children. Among the Indians, for several years, she was not treated unkindly. Once she was rescued from the death-hug of a bear, and at another time she had nearly drowned; "But," says she, "surely the Saviour remembered that I should so much like to live and die with the Brethren." In 1757, to her infinite joy, she was taken by three chiefs to Philadelphia, where, as a result of a treaty of peace, she was set at liberty, finding a home in a kind Quaker family. During her stay with them a man who had "dreamed" that she was his kidnapped child came to the city, claimed her, and, following the decision of a magistrate, took her, despite her denial of him, with him to Lancaster. "My continual prayer," she writes, "was that the good Lord would restore me to my true parents; and He heard me, too." To the Synod of 1758, convened in Lancaster, came her father and mother; they heard of the child, went to see her, there was mutual recognition, a dispute with the pretended father, and, finally, recourse to a Justice of the Peace who said to the Schmidts, "Take her, for flesh and blood will not be denied!" Then the happy parents with their child repaired to the "school-house" (in West Orange St.) where they were presented to the assembled synod and congregation by Brother Joseph (Spangenberg) who, taking Christina by the hand, asked her father and mother, "Will you give this child to the Saviour and the

Brethren?" So, after a visit to her Maryland home, she joined the Sisters' "Choir" in Bethlehem. In 1770, because of ill-health, consumption, she was transferred to the Sisters' House in Lititz, so that she might have the medical attention of Dr. Fahnestock of Ephrata; then came a temporary restoration, a recurrence, and death in her twenty-eighth year.

32. **Sarah Delker.** I, l. xi, 5. Nov. 24. Unmarried Sister. Born in Dornhan, Wuertemberg, Sept. 7, 1748.

1775.

33. **John Andrew Blickensderfer.** I, r. x, 3. Jan. 10. Unmarried. Oldest son of Christian and Catharina Blickensderfer. Born April 18, 1750, in the village of Lower Saucheim in the Palatinate.

34. **Eva Barbara Tshudy,** m.n. Kiesel. I, l. xix, 3. March 7. Wife of Christian Tshudy. Born at Muddy Creek, Nov. 23, 1746. Died of diphtheria, then epidemic.

35. **John Ernst Scheffel.** I, r. xiv, 4. March 28. Young son of Ernst and Catharine Scheffel, born Jan. 28, 1765. Died of diphtheria.

36. **Peter Williard.** I, r. x, 4. April 17. Unmarried. Born in Manocasy, Md., Feb. 4, 1751. Tanner's apprentice with Brother Geitner.

37. **Anna Barbara Yungblut.** I, l. xi, 6. April 19. Unmarried Sister. Born in Bethel on the Swatara, May 16, 1751.

1776.

38. **Gottfried Roesler.** I, r. xix, 3. Jan. 6. Born April 11, 1711, in Neustadt near Dresden, Saxony. Came to Pennsylvania in 1750. Ordained a Deacon of the Church in 1759, at the Synod in Lancaster. Served at Donegal, Hebron, Warwick and in other country congregations. His last seven years were spent in Lititz as schoolmaster for the Warwick boys. Married Marianne Mueller. They had two children, twins, who died soon after birth. On the morning of Jan. 6, as he was returning from a country visit, he was stricken with sudden death and fell, as he was found, by the roadside, his face imbedded in the snow. His funeral was largely attended, for, "because of his fine school" he was respected and loved by old and young.

39. **Christian Thomas.** I, r. x, 5. Feb. 4. Unmarried. Born in Lancaster, Nov. 1, 1754, and came with his parents John and Maria Salome (m.n. Gorner) Thomas to Lititz in 1759. Exceptionally talented in music, he was the first organist of the Lititz congregation. Died of miliary fever.

40. **Hans Christopher Christensen.** I, r. x, 6. Sept. 15. Unmarried. Born Feb. 7, 1716, near Hadersleben, Holstein. Joined the Moravians, in Herrnhut, 1745. Came to Bethlehem, 1751. An expert mill-wright and hydraulic engineer, he built the first oil-mill and the water-works in Bethlehem; a grist and saw-mill in Bethabara, N. C.; the same for Hope, N. J., and, besides many more, the first grist and saw-mill in Lititz, in 1757. Upon hearing of the total destruction by fire, in 1775, of the latter, he volunteered his services, although in an

advanced stage of consumption, to build a new one (which is still standing); and this he accomplished, but at such expense of his waning strength that he was constrained to take a bed in the infirmary of the Brethren's House, and there he died.

41. **Margaretha Elizabeth Grubé,** m.n. Krieger. 1, l. xx, 2. Nov. 10. Born Nov. 12, 1716, at Reval, Livonia. In 1754 she was married to Joachim Busse, going with him to Herrnhut and uniting with the Moravians. Together they went, 1751, as missionaries to St. Thomas, where her husband died, leaving her with eight children, of whom Andrew Busse (once pastor in Nazareth) was the eldest. In the same year she came to Bethlehem, and in 1755 was married to Bernhard Adam Grubé, with whom she served in the Indian missions of Gnadenhuetten, Pachgatgoch and Wechquetank, and accompanied the Moravian Indians into exile, for safety, to Province Island, and, subsequently, to the "Barracks" in Philadelphia. During these missionary years she suffered hardships innumerable. In Pachgatgoch, for instance, the winter night was so bitterly cold in their wigwam, that to save her baby's life she must make its sleeping place between two great Indian dogs. In May, 1765, they were called to Lititz, her husband to be co-pastor with Bishop Hehl and have the superintendence of the congregation schools; also to organize a choir and church orchestra. For eleven years she served as Spiritual Overseer of the married Sisters. They had one daughter, Anna Johanna, who married the Rev. John Martin Beck. Her final illness was caused by exposure to extremely inclement weather as she came, in an open conveyance, from a visit in Bethlehem to Lititz. Her husband wrote of her "She was a woman of much experience."

42. **Susanna Michler.** 1, l. xx, 3. Dec. 9. Born March 15, 1722, in Wildberg, Würtemberg. United with the Brethren at Marienborn, 1743. There she was married to John George Ohneberg, coming, same year, with him to Bethlehem. In 1744 they moved to Nazareth, where, in the economy of that time, they superintended the clearing of the land and establishing of the farms. In 1748 they had charge of the school in Macungie (Emmaus) and later that of Lancaster. Received a call, 1750, as missionaries to St. Thomas, W. I., and then to St. Croix. Returned to Bethlehem, 1760, where her husband died. They had fifteen children. In 1762 she married Rev. John Michler, served with him in the school in Nazareth Hall, and then they were called, she for the second time, to the West India mission, Jamaica. Returned, 1770, and served in Heidelberg, Pa. In 1776 they sought retirement in Lititz, and here she died.

1777.

43. **Peter Mordick.** 1, r. x, 7. Jan. 19. Unmarried. Born in Nazareth Sept. 7, 1755. Nailsmith. Died, a patient sufferer, of an epidemic pectoral fever.

44. **Elias Glotz.** 1, r. xix, 2. Feb. 18. Born Dec. 7, 1745; oldest son of Albrecht and Margaretha (m.n. Rieth, of Tulpehockon) Glotz. Em-

ployed on the farm of John Henry Haller, whose daughter Elizabeth he married. No children.

45. **Anna Maria Shank.** 1, l. xi, 7. Feb. 26. Unmarried Sister. Born Jan. 24, 1749, in Upper Kiepingen, Würtemberg. Came, in her fourth year, with her parents, to this country. In her fifteenth year she was "awakened" by the personal persuasion of David Zeisberger, giving him "her hand to it" to remain true to the Saviour. Came to Lititz, 1768, engaged in domestic service in Jasper Payne's family, and in 1770 moved into the Sisters' House, where she died of consumption.

46. **Elizabeth Beck.** 1, l. x, 7. Sept. 4. Unmarried Sister. A daughter of the Rev. Henry Beck, she was born in Bethlehem, Oct. 11, 1746. Came in 1763 to the Lititz Sisters' House. Superintendent of the weaving department. Died of consumption.

47. **Anna Maria Hehl.** 1, l. xx, 1. Nov. 22. Beloved wife of Bishop Matthew Hehl. Born in Berthelsdorf, Upper Lusatia, Nov. 17, 1716. Her parents were Christopher and Helena (m. n. Henk) Jaehne, descendants of Moravian exiles. Spiritually awakened in the children's revival of 1727, in Herrnhut. In 1733, in her seventeenth year, previously confirmed in Herrnhut, she partook for the first time of the Lord's Supper, and was blessed by Pastor Rothe, in the church of Berthelsdorf. In 1737, Nov. 17, she was married to Matthew Hehl who, while she had charge of the girls in the Herrnhut Orphanage, served in the same situation for the boys. Three children were born to them: John and Johanna Maria, both dying in infancy, and Mathew Leonhard, born in Herrnhut, in 1749. In August, 1751, they received their call to Pennsylvania. Leaving their little son at school in Barby—he rejoined them after nineteen years—they sailed from London, arriving in Bethlehem, Dec. 10. In November, 1756, they came to Lititz, Bro. Hehl a newly-consecrated bishop of the Brethren's Church. She died of a pectoral fever on the fortieth anniversary of their marriage.

48. **Catharina Volck.** 1, l. x, 6. Dec. 12. Unmarried Sister. Born April 2, 1743, in Lynn, Pa.

1778.

49. **John Jacob Schmick.** 1, r. xx, 2. Jan. 23. Presbyter. Born Oct. 19, 1714, at Koenigsberg, Prussia. While in charge of a Lutheran congregation in Livonia, he became acquainted with the Moravians and united with them in 1748. Came to Bethlehem in 1751, destined for service in the Indian mission. 1752, ordained a Deacon of the Church. Ordained a presbyter in 1759. Married Johanna Ingerheidt. With his wife he labored in various missions. A proficient in the Mohican language, and adopted by the Shawanese into their nation. Was with the Christian Indians in exile, for safety, in Philadelphia, and, after their release, led them to Wyalusing. His last mission was at Gnadenhuetten, Ohio. In August, 1777, he came to Lititz, and was appointed an assistant to Bishop Hehl, while his wife became the Spiritual Overseer of the Married Sisters.

When, in December, the U. S. military hospital was established in the Brethren's House, he preached faithfully to the wretched soldiery; and there he contracted the "camp-fever" of which he died. One son, John Jacob, survived him; two daughters preceded him into eternity.

50. **Catharina Blickensderfer,** m.n. Sherzer. 1, l. xix, 4. Jan. 27. Born Oct. 14, 1727, in Eisenbach, Rhenish Bavaria. Married Christian Blickensderfer, and came with him and two children, first to Philadelphia, where they lived one and a half years, and then to a farm near Lititz. In 1761 they built a house in the village and moved into it. Of her nine children two sons and a daughter survived her. Died of the epidemic "camp-fever."

51. **Henry Oerter.** 1, r. xii, 2. Jan. 31. Born in Bethlehem, April 10, 1752; second son of Christian Frederick Oerter, and twin-brother of Anna Oerter. Unmarried. Came to Lititz, 1775, to take charge of the Brethren's smithy. Died of the epidemic "camp-fever."

52. **Christopher Pohl.** 1, r. xii, 1. Feb. 1. Unmarried. Born Jan. 6, 1724, in Habendorf, Lower Silesia. Came to Lititz, 1759, and here he was for nineteen years cook in the Brethren's House. Died of the epidemic "camp-fever."

53. **Elizabeth Michler.** 1, l. x, 5. March 13. Unmarried Sister. Born on the Island of St. Thomas, where her parents were missionaries, April 4, 1756.

54. **Elizabeth Ricksecker,** m.n. Krieger. 1, l. xix, 5. Sept. 3. Wife of Peter Ricksecker. Born Dec. 2, 1751, in Manocasy, Md. Had two children, a son and a daughter. Died four hours after the birth of the latter.

1779.

56. **Matthew Baumgaertner.** 1, r. xx, 3. April 19. Born in Switzerland, Oct. 6, 1708. Settled in Donegal, but, in 1758, having fled for safety from the Indians to Lititz, he received permission to remain here. By his first wife he had one daughter, Catharina; by the second (m.n. Goepfert) he had twelve children, six surviving him.

57. **Maria Elizabeth Ricksecker.** 1, l. xiii, 3. June 5. Infant daughter of Peter Ricksecker (at the fulling-mill). Aged 9 months.

58. **Jasper Payne.** 1, r. xx, 4. July 3. Born April 23, 1708, in Twickenham, England. Came in 1743 with his wife and aged mother to Bethlehem, where he was made steward of the Economy. Ordained a Deacon of the Church, 1753. Served several years in Philadelphia, but for the most part, labored in the Gospel in the rural churches. In 1767 he came to Lititz to take charge of the congregation store. By his second wife (m.n. Philippina Way, of New London, Conn.) he had two sons, Jasper and Nathaniel, both surviving him.

59. **Johanna Rosina Rauch.** 1, l. xiii, 4. Jan. 11. Infant of John Henry and Catharine Rauch.

1780.

60. **Catherine Toon.** 1, l. x, 4. Jan. 11. Unmarried Sister. Born March 9, 1761. A poor, homeless and consumptive girl of eighteen years,

she endeavored, in June, 1799, to make her way, as best she might, from Carroll's Manor, Maryland, to Lititz, where she hoped to be received into the Sisters' House, her half-sister Mary Tippet, being one of that "choir." Arrived at an inn in Taneytown, with seventy more miles to go, the landlord kindly allowed her to remain there for a short time in the hope that some passing conveyance might take her farther on her way. "After a few days, Col. Curtis Grubb came in his coach to the inn. I begged him to take me with him to the neighborhood of Lancaster, but he refused me point-blank, saying that he could not drag a sick woman about with him. Then, upon my further entreaty, he asked me, 'Well, where, near Lancaster, do you wish to go?' To Lititz, to my sister, said I. 'Have you a sister in Lititz—and does she belong to the Brethren? Well, then I will take you with me.' During the whole journey he treated me with the tenderness of a father; would not allow me to pay for anything, and ordered for me such delicacies as were best adapted to my enfeebled condition. He repeatedly assured me, in words of kind encouragement, how happy I should be if I obtained leave to live with the Brethren and Sisters at Lititz, for he knew them to be true children of God. When we were come four miles from Lititz where his homeward way led off from the Lititz road, (at Neffsville, via Manheim for Mt. Hope) he gave me a letter he had written to Bro. Andrew Horn (landlord of *Zum Anker* Inn near Lititz) to insure my good reception with him; placed me in the care of his secretary for the remaining distance, and then, at parting with me, pressed into my hand a beautiful piece of gold. Oh, God, reward him for his kindness!"

61. **John Renatus Christ.** 1, r. xiv, 5. Jan. 21. Infant son of Peter and Juliana Christ.

62. **Anna Magdalena Meyer.** 1, l. x, 3. April 6. Unmarried Sister. Born in Ulm, May 1, 1710. Came to Lititz, 1762, to be the first *Pflegerin* (Spiritual Overseer) in the new Sisters' House; but in 1764 she was superseded in this office by Sr. Augustine and given that of Warden of her "choir," a position which she filled admirably for sixteen years to her end.

63. **Maria Kreiter,** m.n. Hirschy. 1, l. xix, 6. Aug. 31. Born in Hempfield Township, 1728. Wife of Peter Kreiter. They moved to Lititz in 1770. Eight children, all of whom survived her.

64. **Anna Dorothea Glotz.** 1, l. x, 2. Sept. 19. Unmarried Sister. Consumption.

1781.

65. **John George Ohneberg.** 1, r. xii, 4. April 24. Unmarried. Born on the Island of St. Croix, Dec. 19, 1751.

66. **Rosina Christ.** 1, l. xiii, 5. May 24. Daughter of Peter Christ, aged four years and nine months. Her death was caused by the lodgement of a bean in her windpipe.

67. **Christian Henry Werner.** 1, r. xiv, 6. May 26. Born in Lititz, 1775.

68. **Anna Christina Francke,** m.n. Bezold. 1, l. xx, 4. June 14. Wife of
Rev. John Chistopher Francke. Born Oct. 28, 1713, in Halle,
Saxony. Came to Lititz, 1763. Of three sons and four daughters
only John Immanuel and Agnes survived her.

69. **Anna Maria Cassler.** 1, l. x, 1. Sept. 17. Unmarried Sister. Born
in Lititz, April 1, 1761. Daughter of Lewis and Christina Cassler.

70. **Adolph Meyer.** 1, r. xx, 5. Oct. 6. Physician and surgeon to the
Lititz congregation. Born in Westerhausen, Saxony, March 15,
1714. Learned his profession from his father. United with the
Brethren in Herrnhut, 1736. In 1739 he married Mary Dorothea
Cartaus, and received a call to Pennsylvania. His wife, because of
sickness, could not accompany him; later she sailed for America
but died off the Banks of Newfoundland and was buried at sea
Arrived in Philadelphia, Dr. Meyer was sent to Nazareth where he
practiced medicine and was the first Elder of the congregation. In
1745 he married Maria Justina Kraft, and in 1746 they were called
to take charge of the Boys' School in Fredericktown, remaining in
that situation until the close of 1749. Because of Sr. Meyer's continual ill-health, they asked for their release and began housekeep-
ing for themselves, Dr. Meyer serving his neighborhood with his
medical and surgical knowledge. "Our attachment to the Congregation was never lessened, and although we did not visit it, we, as was
the case with the Prophet Daniel, never lost our remembrance of
or our longing for it." At that time his son Christian—a bright
young man—died. "Visited by the Brethren, their kind love melted
my heart, and made us long to live again in a *Gemein-ort*" (Congregation settlement). Therefore they were appointed to Lititz, and
came hither June 6, 1776.

71. **Samuel Krause.** 1, r. xii, 5. Oct. 22. Unmarried. Born in Nazareth,
Nov. 22, 1749. Master of domestic affairs in the Brethren's House.
Died of an epidemic fever.

1782.

72. **Maria Van Vleck,** m.n. Schmidt. 1, l. xix, 7. Jan. 27. Born in Bethlehem, April 24, 1752. First wife of Henry Van Vleck (hatter).

73. **John Renatus Keller.** 1, r. xii, 6. Feb. 22. Unmarried. Born Aug.
23, 1727. In 1773 he was ordained a Deacon of the church and then
received a call to Pennsylvania, coming the same year to Lititz.
Warden of the Single Brethren's "choir." Died of consumption.

74. **Elizabeth Ricksecker.** 1, l. xii, 7. May 7. Unmarried Sister. Born
in Warwick, 1762. Daughter of Peter Ricksecker.

75. **John Christopher Francke.** 1, r. xii, 7. Aug. 22. Born in Schnee-
berg, Saxony, Dec. 30, 1711. Converted by the preaching of Zinzendorf in Berlin. Married Anna Christina Bezold. Came to this
country, 1742. Director of the Boys' Schools in Nazareth, Fredericktown, Oley and Macungie. Ordained a Deacon of the Church,
1749. In Lititz, from 1763, he and his wife had the superintendence of
the married "choir" and he was the congregation's Warden. He was
stricken with apoplexy while sitting, as president, at a meeting of

the *Aufseher Collegium* (Committee of Temporal Affairs), dying soon afterwards.

76. **Sophia Dorothea Gattermeyer.** I, l. xii, 6. Aug. 29. Unmarried Sister. Born in Bethlehem, Jan. 19, 1751. Her father, John Gattermeyer, was killed by the Indians in the massacre at Gnadenhuetten on the Mahony, 1755. Consumption.

77. **Margaretha Kling.** I, l. xii, 5. Nov. 13. Unmarried Sister. Born in Donegal, Pa., 1737. Employed in the bakery of the Sisters' House and was mistress of its dairy.

78. **John Gottfried Zahm.** I, r. xii, 7. Dec. 19. Unmarried. Born in Bethlehem, May 10, 1753. Came in 1779 to Lititz as *Pfleger* (Spiritual Overseer) of the Single Brethren. Both he and his second in authority, (Renatus Keller, Warden, No. 73) were remarkably successful in their calling with the young men. They lie side by side on the graveyard. A fine musician. Ordained a Deacon of the Church a few months before his death. Consumption.

1783.

79. **Catharine Rauch,** m.n. Gutjahr. I, l. xviii, 1. Jan. 2. Born in Lancaster, Feb. 3, 1747. First wife of John Henry Rauch. Consumption.

80. **Martha, an Indian.** I, l. xii, 4. March 20. Unmarried Sister. Born in Shecomeko, 1739. Her parents were Thomas and Esther, Mohicans. Baptized by Christian Henry Rauch. 1748, was servitress in the Germantown Moravian School; 1763-64, in exile with the Christian Indians in Philadelphia. Came in 1771 to Lititz to be the mistress-tailoress in the Sisters' House. Served, also, several years as a teacher in the congregation day-school for girls.

81. **Dorothea Klein,** m.n. Davis. I, l. xviii, 2. July 23. Born Aug. 28, 1721, "on the Schuylkill." Was converted by Zinzendorf when he, with other Brethren, lodged in her brother-in-law's barn. Her third husband was George Klein, popularly known as the founder of Lititz. Lived in Bethlehem, but came to Lititz to have the treatment of Dr. Fahnestock, of Ephrata, for a cancerous affection about her head. Somewhat improved she returned to her home, but, her malady increasing again, she came back to Lititz to have her physician's care until her death, which she knew to be inevitable. About the time of her funeral an express came to Lititz with the news of her husband's death in Bethlehem. (George Klein and his first wife, Anna, m.n. Bender, both came from Kirchardt in the Palatinate. In 1754 he donated 491 acres of land to the Lititz Congregation, receiving from the church an annuity of £70 during his life).

82. **John Paul Hennig.** I, r. xii, 8. Aug. 21. Unmarried. Born Jan. 1, 1715, of Roman Catholic parents. United with the Moravians in Herrnhaag, 1743. Came to this country in 1750, and was employed in the Economy at Christianspring as cook, and also as a teacher of the boys. To Lititz in 1767 as master-shoemaker in the Brethrens' House.

83. **Dorothea Rosina Horn,** m.n. Fischer. 1, l. xviii, 3. Oct. 18. Born in Lower Silesia, Sept. 3, 1713. Wife of Bro. Andrew Horn.
84. **Elizabeth Peter,** m.n. Koehler. 1, l. xviii, 4. Dec. 18. Born in Macungie (Emmaus) Sept. 11, 1749. Wife of Bro. Simon Peter. Consumption.

1784.

85. **Frederick Peter.** 1, r. xiv, 7. March 11. Infant son of Simon and Elizabeth Peter.
86. **John Nathaniel Danz.** 1, r. xiv, 8. July 31. Infant son of Simon Danz.
87. **Marie Magdalena Augustine.** 1, l. xii, 3. May 23. Unmarried Sister. Born in Gotha, Thuringia, Aug. 3, 1714. After much varied service in European congregations she, in 1763, sailed with Capt. Jacobson in the "Hope" from Gravesend for New York, having a calm and delightful voyage; and thence came directly to Lititz whither she had been called, and where she continued until her death the very distinguished *Pflegerin* of the Sisters' "choir." She was also the General Superintendent of the Single Sisters in America.
88. **Henry Frey.** 1, r. xx, 6. Sept. 25. Born May 12, 1724, in Falckner's Swamp. Converted by the preaching of Christian Henry Rauch, he united with the Moravians in 1744. Destined for the Indian mission he learned the Maqua language from Bro. Pyrlaeus. Accompanied David Zeisberger on his journey to Onondaga. Maried Anna Maria Buerstler. Served the Church in various capacities; was the Warden of Nazareth Congregation; and finally came to Lititz where, for a few years, he was the miller, and then moved up into the village to work at his trade of carpentry. When the mill was destroyed by fire in 1775, he as master-carpenter superintended the building of the new (present) one.
89. **Anna Maria Frey.** 1, l. xviii, 5. Sept. 27. Born in Oley, Feb. 23, 1730. Wife of Henry Frey.
90. **Anna Maria Protzman.** 1, l. xviii, 6. Nov. 3. Born Sept. 23, 1723, in Waechtersbach, near Herrnhaag. Wife of John Ludwig Protzmann, who died in 1778. Epidemic fever. She had five sons and three daughters. Nine grandchildren.
91. **Beata Rauch.** 1, l. xiii, 6. Nov. 12. Infant daughter of John Henry Rauch.

1785.

92. **John Michler.** 1, r. xx, 7. June 20. Born Oct. 24, 1720, in Leuchingen, Wuertemberg. Served in the boys' schools of Nazareth and Fredericktown and twice as a missionary in the West Indies. His second wife was Margaret Roseen, m.n. Rieth; his third the Widow Ohneberg; his fourth, Margaret Sherger. Died of an epidemic fever.
93. **Susanna Maria Kreiter.** 1, l. xiii, 7. July 3. Daughter of Peter Kreiter. Aged two years.

94. **Anna Catharina Fertig,** m.n. Seidner. 1, l. xviii, 7. Aug. 23. Born in Wertheim, Germany, Sept. 24, 1723. Her husband, John Christopher Fertig, and she had charge of the Lititz church farm.
95. **Joseph Willey.** 1, r. xi, 8. Sept. 30. Unmarried. Born May 3, 1731, in Okenshaw, Yorkshire, England. United with the Moravians at Fulneck. Master weaver in the Lititz Brethren's House.
96. **Beatus Hanke.** 1, r. xiv, 9. Dec. 8.

1786.

97. **John Matthew Kreiter.** 1, r. xii, 9. Jan. 3. Unmarried. Born near Lititz, Dec. 24, 1760. Son (sixth) of Peter and Maria (Hirschy) Kreiter. Consumption.
98. **Regina Kreiter,** m.n. Fertig. 1, l. xvii, 1. Feb. 8. Wife of Andrew Kreiter, fulling-miller. Born Dec. 27, 1755, in Wertheim, Germany.
99. **Anna Ricksecker,** m.n. Meyer. 1, l. xvii, 2. April 24. Born in Ueberschimmerhof, near Worms, March 5, 1720. Her first husband was Henry Schneider, of Donegal; her second, Peter Ricksecker, Sr., of Warwick. Both the latter and she contracted the "camp-fever" in 1778; she recovered but he died of it.
100. **Andrew Horn.** 1, r. xx, 8. Nov. 4. Born March 8, 1717, in Eichenbach, Würtemberg. United with the Brethren in Herrnhut, 1742. Came to Pennsylvania 1744, and with his wife, Dorothea Rosina, m.n. Fischer, served the Bethlehem Economy in various ways. Ordained a Deacon of the Church, 1755. Came to Lititz, 1761; was Warden of the congregation, an always useful member of the *Aufseher Collegium,* and, finally, the first and very popular landlord of the Congregation's tavern *"Zum Anker"* (present Lititz Springs Hotel). His remains were the first to lie in the new (present) corpse-house.
101. **Christina Elizabeth Glotz.** 1, l. xii, 2. Nov. 23. Unmarried Sister. Born in Lititz, 1765. Consumption.

1787.

102. **Maria Dorothea Lecron.** 1, l. xii, 1. Feb. 9. Unmarried Sister. Born in Cocalico Township, Jan. 14, 1752.
103. **Maria Justina Meyer.** 1, l. xvii, 3. April 29. Wife of Dr. Adolph Meyer. Consumption.
104. **Louisa Danz.** 1, l. xiii, 8. June 21. Aged 3 months.
105. **John William Werner.** 1, r. xix, 8. June 24. Born March 1, 1722, in Manheim, in the Palatinate. Came to this country 1744. His first wife's maiden name was Blum; they had three daughters. Second marriage was to Sr. Schuchard, three sons and two daughters; his third, to Anna Maria Kiesel—three sons and one daughter. By trade a cooper, he was also the village phlebotomist and tooth-drawer.
106. **Jacob August Danz.** 1, r. xiv, 10. July 15. Aged 4 months.
107. **Sarah Van Vleck.** 1, l. xiv, 8. Aug. 11. Infant daughter of Henry Van Vleck.

243

108. **Catharine Blickensderfer.** 1, l. xiii, 9. Sept. 20. Aged 3 years.
109. **Catharine Glotz,** m.n. Born. 1, l. xvii, 4. Oct. 4. Born in Rhenish
    Bavaria, March 15, 1733. Wife of Albrecht Glotz. One son and
    two daughters. Consumption.
110. **Matthew Godfrey Hehl,** Episcopus Fratrum. 1, r. xx, 1. Dec. 4.
    Born April 30, 1705, at Ebersdorf, Würtemberg. Received the
    degree of Master of Arts in 1723 at the University of Tuebingen.
    By the influence of Christian David, and, subsequently, that of
    Zinzendorf, he was led to unite with the Moravians. In 1737 he
    married Anna Maria Jaehne (see No. 47). Arrived in Bethlehem,
    1751. Came in 1756 to Lititz where he was for twenty-eight years
    the principal pastor and Superintendent of a circuit of Moravian
    churches in this diocese, of which Lititz was the centre. A profound
    theologian, an eloquent preacher, a gifted musician and a fine
    hymnologist, he ranked in usefulness to the Moravian Church with
    the foremost leaders of his time. The inscription upon his grave-
    stone reads as follows:

> Matthaeus
> Gottfried Hehl
> Tübingensis
> gebr. in Würtemberg
> d. 30 April 1705
> verschied 4 Dec. 1787
> seines Alters 82 Jahre
> seines Episcopats
> 37 Jahre

1788.

111. **Maria Barbara Leinbach.** 1, l. xii, 8. Jan. 18. Unmarried Sister.
112. **Sophia Christ.** 1, l. xiv, 9. Feb. 12. Aged 10 months.
113. **John George Lehnert.** 1, r. xiv, 2. Aged 8 months.
114. **Elizabeth Van Vleck,** m.n. Riem. 1, l. xvii, 5. Feb. 18. Second
    wife of Henry Van Vleck, hatter. Born in Lancaster, Sept. 14, 1758.
115. **Anna Christina Zander.** 1, l. xi, 8. March 19. Unmarried Sister.
    Born in Berbice, South America, Oct 6, 1749.
116. **Anna Susanna Born,** m.n. Leuthold. 1, l. xvii, 6. June 6. Born
    Sept. 1733, in Berne, Switzerland. A widow.
117. **Samuel Tannenberg.** 1, r. x 8. June 17. Born in Lititz, April 23,
    1766. Unmarried. Son of David Tannenberg.
118. **Joseph Hobsch.** 1, r. xi, 9. July 4. Unmarried. Born in Schoen-
    heide, Silesia, Jan. 17, 1715.
119. **Abraham Frederick.** 1, r. xviii, 1. Oct. 16. Born in Donegal, July
    11, 1723. Married.
120. **Godfrey Aust.** 1, r. xviii, 2. Oct. 28. Born April 5, 1722. From
    Salem, N. C.
121. **Jacob Tshudy.** 1, r. x, 9. Dec. 21. Unmarried. Born in Lititz,
    Aug. 22, 1766. Son of Christian and Eva Barbara (Kiesel) Tshudy.

1789.

122. **Simon Danz.** 1, r. xviii, 3. Jan. 19. Born in Switzerland, April 11, 1744. Married. Landlord of *"Zum Anker"* Inn.

123. **Anna Johanna Ricksecker.** 1, l. x, 8. Jan. 20. Unmarried Sister. Born Jan. 15, 1759.

124. **Beatus Lennert.** 1, r. xiv, 12. Feb. 20.

125. **John Peter Lennert.** 1, r. xiv, 13. Feb. 26. Twin-brother of the last named. Sons of Peter Lennert.

126. **Sarah Denke,** m.n. Test. 1, l. xx, 5. May 3. Born June 28, 1789. Superintendent of the Married Sisters. Second wife of Rev. Jeremiah Denke, pastor in Lititz.

127. **Georgina Elizabeth Proske.** 1, l. xii, 9. Aug. 29. Unmarried Sister. Born in Jamaica, W. I., Jan. 10, 1764. Consumption.

128. **Albrecht Glotz.** 1, r. xviii, 4. Dec. 9. Born Nov. 27, 1714, in Franconia. Tobacconist.

1790.

129. **Elizabeth Burnet.** 1, l. xi, 9. April 4. Unmarried Sister. Born in New York, July 16, 1730. Teacher in the Girl's School.

130. **Benigna Eichler.** 1, l. xvii, 7. May 17. Born Dec. 28, 1768, in Lititz. Daughter of Albrecht Glotz. Wife of Gottlieb Eichler.

131. **John Daniel Sydrich.** 1, r. xviii, 5. May 22. Presbyter. Born May 1, 1727, in Frankfort-on-the-Main. His father was Hieronymus Sydrich, a confectioner; mother's maiden name was Abt. After his father's death he went with his mother to Herrnhut—he to live in the Orphanage where he had the ever valued instruction of Bro. Matthew Hehl, its Director, in the languages and sciences. Came to Bethlehem in 1750. Served in the Boys' Schools of Emmaus and Christianspring, going from the latter place occasionally to preach in Shoeneck. Ordained as Deacon, 1760. Married Gertrude Peterson, 1774. Labored in Philadelphia, Hope, N. J., in the Brethren's House in Lititz, and at Graceham, his favorite and last congregation. On May 8, although in very ill-health, he came to Lititz as a member of a synod, at which he was ordained a presbyter, but died soon afterward, May 27. Sr. Sydrich writes of him that "he loved and was loved in return."

132. **Eva Barbara Christ.** 1, l. xvii, 8. June 3. Born in Hempfield Township, Sept. 21, 1746. Daughter of Valentine Grosh. Wife of Daniel Christ. Had five children; Christian, John, Maria Catharine and Susanna. Maria survived her.

133. **Christian David Kreiter.** 1, r. xii, 10. June 5. Unmarried. Born April 5, 1765; a son of Peter Kreiter.

134. **Maria Barbara Geitner.** 1, l. xviii, 8. July 16. Born Jan. 13, 1726, in Hoff, Voigtland. In Bethlehem, 1762, she married the widower John George Geitner and, in 1767, moved with him to Lititz. For her children see No. 138.

1791.

135. **Ulrich Daumer.** 1, r. xi, 10. Feb. 2. Unmarried. Shoemaker in the Brethren's House. Aged 67 years.

136. **Henry Daumer.** 1, r. xi, 11. May 13. Unmarried. Same trade in same place. Brother of the foregoing; both from Frankfort-on-the-Main. Aged 74 years, 6 months.

137. **John Michael Bitzman.** 1, r. xii, 11. July 5. Unmarried. Born December 15, 1726, in Bubehausen, Hesse-Darmstadt. Steward in the Brethren's House.

138. **John George Geitner.** 1, r. xviii, 6. Aug. 30. Tanner. Born May 20, 1715, in Zeulenrode, Voigtland. Son of John George Geitner, tanner; his mother's maiden name was Schuler. Came to Bethlehem 1748; married Susanna Dorothea Kraup, who died there in 1760. They had three sons: Christian Gottlieb (died in infancy); John Ludwig, 1757, and John George, born 1760. In 1762 he married Maria Barbara Hendel and came with her to Lititz, 1767. Their children were Maria Barbara (died 1774), and Maria Salome, born 1766.

139. **George Michael Kreiter.** 1, r. xiii, 1. Sept. 23. Son of Michael Gottfried Kreiter. Aged one year.

140. **Margaret Becker.** 1, l. xvii, 9. Oct. 27. Born April 4, 1737, in the Palatinate. Daughter of Valentine Grosh. Wife of John Becker, store-keeper. One son, John Leonhard, survived her.

141. **Maria Christine Ranck.** 1, l. xii, 10. Oct. 30. Unmarried Sister. Born Nov. 17, 1765, she was the second daughter of Philip and Anna Barbara (m.n. Stauffer) Ranck.

142. **Jacob Augustus Lennert.** 1, r. xiii, 2. Jan. 3. Infant son of Peter Lennert.

1792.

143. **Anna Rosina Tannenberg,** m.n. Kern. 1, l. xx, 6. Feb. 17. Born in Ebersdorf, Upper Lusatia, 1763. Wife of the organ-builder David Tannenberg (colloquially, and usually written, Tanneberger). (He came with his family to Lititz in 1765, having purchased the *"Pilgerhaus"* for a residence and manufactory. His organs stood in high repute, and were ordered from Philadelphia, Baltimore, Albany, Lancaster and many more places. In 1804, as he was tuning a new organ he had built for the Lutheran Church in York, he suffered an attack of apoplexy of which, after a few days, he died. Buried in York). Their children were Rosina, married William Cassler; Maria Elizabeth, married John Schropp; Anna Maria, married Philip Bachman; David, and Samuel.

144. **Thomas Kreiter.** 1, r. xiii, 3. May 12. Son of Frederick Peter Kreiter. Aged 24 days.

145. **Gertrude Ricksecker.** 1, l. x, 9. May 20. Unmarried Sister. Born March 16, 1755. Daughter of Peter Ricksecker.

246

1793.

146. **Timotheus Van Vleck.** i, r. xiii, 4. Feb. 9. Son of Henry Van Vleck. Aged 3 years.

147. **John Martin Schmidt.** i, r. x, 10. May 2. Unmarried. Born Sept. 14, 1716. Came to this country, 1761.

148. **Barbara Grosh,** m.n. Sandmann. i, l. xviii, 9. March 15. Widow of John Valentine Grosh. Born in Schorsheim, Palatinate, 1708. Came with her husband to this country, 1743, and to Lititz, 1764. She had twelve children, fifty grandchildren and five great-grand-children.

149. **Catharine Brinckman.** i, l. xi, 10. July 7. Unmarried Sister. Born in York, Feb. 3, 1760.

150. **Elizabeth Mueller.** i, l. xiii, 10. Sept. 11. Daughter of John Mueller. Aged 5 years.

151. **George Sturgis.** i, r. x, 11. Sept. 15. Born in Lebanon, 1775, a son of Joseph Sturgis. Linen-weaver.

1794.

152. **Anna Maria Kreiter,** m.n. Thomas. i, l. xix, 8. Apil 9. Born in Lititz, Oct. 21, 1763. Daughter of John Thomas, baker, and wife of John Kreiter.

153. **Margaretha Schenck.** i, l. x, 10. Aug. 31. Unmarried Sister. Born in Lancaster, Jan. 31, 1767. Came to Lititz and moved into the Sister's House, 1785.

154. **Rebecca Westhaefer.** i, l. (One of two unmarked graves). Sept. 3. Infant daughter of Jacob Westhaefer.

1795.

155. **Beatus Harry.** i, r. xiii, 5. Feb. 20.

156. **Anna Bernhardina (Coelln) Harry.** i, l. xix, 9. Feb. 22. Born in Lititz, June 6, 1769. Daughter of Claus Coelln. Wife of Isaac Renatus Harry.

157. **William Kreiter.** i, r. xiii, 6. Aug. 8. Twin brother of Mary Kreiter (158). Both were baptized and died a few hours after their birth. Children of Michael Christian Kreiter.

158. **Mary Kreiter.** i, l. xiv, 10. Aug. 8.

159. **Anna Christina Rauch,** m.n. Stohler. i, l. xvii, 10. Aug. 13. Wife of John Henry Rauch. Born in Donegal, Dec. 12, 1751. For her children, see 167.

160. **Margaretha Grosh,** m.n. Fried. i, l. xviii, 10. Aug. 25. Born near Wertheim, Franconia, Sept. 29, 1734. Her first husband was George Schenck with whom she had thirteen children; her second was John Grosh—no children.

161. **Anna Salome Blickensderfer.** i, l. xiv, 11. Dec. 12. Daughter of Christian Blickensderfer, Jr. Aged 11 weeks.

162. **Michael Gottfried Kreiter.** i, r. xviii, 7. Dec. 12. Born Jan. 12, 1759, in Hempfield Township, a son of Peter and Maria (Hirschy) Kreiter. Married Maria Magdalena Grosh. Their children were

John, 1786; Jacob, 1788; George Michael, 1790; Gottfried, 1792, and Michael (posthumous), 1795.

163. **Catharine Urich,** m.n. Koerber. 1, l. xix, 10. Dec. 18.

1796.

164. **Maria Michler,** m.n. Scherger. 1, l. xx, 7. May 8. Born in Eisenbach, Rhenish Bavaria, Dec. 10, 1731. Third wife of the Rev. John Michler. No children.

165. **Daniel Ricksecker.** 1, r. xiii, 7. June 26. Lived two days.

166. **Elizabeth Lennert,** m.n. Baumgaertner. 1, l. xx, 8. Aug. 14. Born in Lititz, 1762, a daughter of Matthaeus Baumgaertner. Wife of Peter Lennert, blacksmith. Their children were John George; twin brothers that died directly after birth; Jacob Augustus, and Rebecca, the only one to survive their mother.

167. **John Henry Rauch.** 1, r. xviii, 8. Nov. 11. Spurrier, smith, and auger-maker. Born in Bettingen, Dutchy of Berg, Jan. 21, 1729. Married Catharine Gutjahr, 1755. Their children were Johanna Catharina, 1776; Johanna Rosine, 1779, and Heinrich Gottfried, 1781. His second wife was Anna Christine Stohler, with whom he had the following children: Beata, 1784; John Frederick, 1786; Christian Henry, 1788; John William, 1790, and Maria Christina, 1793, who married Christian David Busse, of Nazareth.

1797.

168. **Maria Barbara Danz.** 1, l. x, 11. Feb. 4. Aged 17 years. Daughter of Simon Danz.

169. **Albrecht Ludolf Russmeyer.** 1, r. xvii, 1. July 4. Presbyter. Labored in Philadelphia, Lancaster, Warwick, Newport, R. I., and New York. He was born in Lueneberg, March 14, 1715, his mother a French-woman, Huguenot. Came to America in 1753, and in 1754 married Maria Evans with whom he had the following children: Peter; the twin-sisters Maria and Elizabeth, 1757; Anna Rebecca, born in Warwick, 1762. Maria married Christian Schropp; the others died in youth.

170. **John George Starck.** 1, r. ix, 1. Aug. 30. Unmarried. Born Nov. 6, 1718. Came to this country 1754. A dyer and stocking manufacturer in the Brethren's House.

1798.

171. **George Frederick Kiesel.** 1, r. xvii, 2. Oct. 6. Born June 13, 1721, in the Palatinate. Came to Warwick, 1729. Married Veronica Leuthold. Had nine children. Farmer.

172. **Rebecca Kreiter.** 1, l. xiii, 12. Oct. 13. Daughter of Michael Christian Kreiter. Aged 1 day.

1799.

173. **Anna Maria Bachman.** 1, l. xx, 9. Feb. 6. Born in Nazareth, 1756, a daughter of David Tannenberg, organ-builder. Married John Philip Bachman. Deranged from melancholia, she drowned herself

3

248

in the streamlet known to Lititz people as the "Little Spring."
No Children.
174. **Anna Elizabeth Ricksecker.** 1, l. xiii, 13. April 2. Born, baptized
and died on the same day.
175. **Beata Tshudy.** 1, l. xiv, 12. April 12. Mathias and Catharine
Tshudy's daughter.
176. **Anton Ronner.** 1, r. xvii, 3. April 15. Born in Philadelphia, 1744.
Tailor. His wife, surviving him, was Christina Michler. Two
children died in their infancy.
177. **Maria Elizabeth Borroway.** 1, l. xi, 11. Aug. 18. Unmarried
Sister. Died in the Sisters' House, aged 25 years. Consumption.
178. **Catharine Barbara Siess.** 1, l. xii, 11. Sept. 1. Born in Heidelberg
on the Tulpehockon, Dec. 27, 1760. Unmarried Sister. Daughter of
John George and Catharine (Lack) Siess. Superintendent of the
larger girls. Died in the Sisters' House of consumption.
179. **Margaret Gutjahr (Goodyear),** m.n. Roesner. 1, l. xx, 10. Dec. 13.
Born 1727, and came in her sixteenth year to this country. Widow
of John Christian Gutjahr. They had five sons and seven daughters;
forty-four grand and two great-grandchildren.
180. **Anna Maria Tshudy.** 1, l. xiv, 13. Dec. 30. A daughter of Christian
Tshudy.

1800.

181. **Christian Blickensderfer, Sr.** 1, r. xvii, 4. April 6. Born near
Manheim, Palatinate, March 6, 1724, of Mennonite parentage. In
1748 he married Catharine Sherger, and came with her and two
children, 1753, to Pennsylvania, settling on a farm near Lititz; and
in 1761 he built a house in the village and moved here. Farmer and
teamster. Of seven sons and two daughters two sons and one
daughter survived him, namely: Christian, 1753, Matthew, 1764, and
Catharine, 1761, who married Matthias Muecke. His second wife,
1779, was the widow Barbara Mueller, m.n. Leuthold, No children.
182. **Susanna Catharine Fetter.** 1, l. xx, 11. July 28. She was born in
Lueneberg, near Halifax, N. S., Oct. 5, 1754. Her maiden name was
Fainot. Came with her parents to Lancaster, where, 1775, she
married John Jacob Fetter. She had four sons and four daughters.
Lived in Warwick.

1801.

183. **Barbara Blickensderfer,** m.n. Kiehler. 1, l. xix, 11. May 1. Born
near Mount Joy, Lancaster Co., Aug. 8, 1764. Wife of Matthew
Blickensderfer. Their children were Jacob, Benjamin, William and
Rosina.
184. **Lisetta Lennert.** 1, l. xiii, 14. May 29. Aged 10 weeks.
185. **Maria Catharine Sommer.** 1, l. xii, 12. Sept. 13. Unmarried Sister.
Born in Hochweisen, Wetteravia, March 11, 1737.
186. **Juliana Busch.** 1, l. xi, 12. Sept. 24. Unmarried Sister. Born in
York, 1765.
187. **Caroline Hall Traeger.** 1, l. xv, 1. Dec. 6. Aged 5 weeks.

1802.

188. **Johanna Salome Lichtenthaeler.** 1, l. xv, 2. Jan. 23. Daughter of Adolph Lichtenthaeler. Aged two years.
189. **Carl Augustus Phillips.** 1, r. xiii, 8. Feb. 4. Aged 1 year, 8 mo.
190. **Andrew Albright.** 1, r. xvii, 5. April 19. He was born at Zella, near Suhl, Thuringia, April 2, 1718. His trade that of gunsmith. A soldier in his youth, he served in the army of Frederick the Great. Came to America, 1750, going to Christianspring to live, and teaching music in the Boys' School at Nazareth. Married Elizabeth Orth, 1766, and until 1767 they had charge of the Sun Inn, at Bethlehem. Came, 1771, to Lititz, where he resumed his trade of gunsmith. He had six children: John, Andrew, John Henry, Jacob, Susanna Elizabeth, wife of Philip Bachman, organ-builder, and Gottfried. He was the tenor singer in the church choir.
191. **Peter Kreiter.** 1, r. xvii, 6. May 10. He was born in Manor Township, near Lancaster, April 12, 1729, a son of Michael (farmer) and Barbara (Grath) Kreiter. Married Maria Hirshy, 1750. Their children were Christian Andrew, 1751; Anna Christina, 1752; Frederick Peter, 1754; Maria Magdalena, 1757; Michael Gottfried, 1759; John Matthew, 1760; Maria Elizabeth, 1763; and Christian David, 1765. His second marriage was to Anna Maria Kohn; their children were Susanna Maria, 1783, and Benjamin, 1786.
192. **Henry Rudy.** 1, r. xvii, 7. June 8. Born in the Black Forest, Würtemberg, Dec. 24, 1708. Farmer, living near Lititz. Married Verona Schnell. Their children were Heinrich Gottlob, John and Christian.
193. **Samuel Christ.** 1, r. xiii, 9. Sept. 5. Son of Daniel Christ, aged two years.
194. **Theresa Christ.** 1, l. xv, 3. Sept. 7. Aged 4 years.

1803.

195. **Beata Westhaefer.** 1, l. xv, 4. Feb. 20.
196. **John Thomas.** 1, r. xvii, 8. March 8. Born in Pfullingen, Würtemberg, Aug. 10, 1727. A baker. Married, in Lancaster, 1749, Maria Salome Gorner. Their children were Rosina, married Andrew Shober, mason; John, Christian, Godfrey, Godfrey (second), Maria Salome, Anna Maria, (married John Renatus Kreiter), and Anna Johanna. His parents were John Peter (farmer) and Margaret (List) Thomas. John Thomas and family came to Lititz, 1759.
197. **Maria Catharine Meyer.** 1, l. x, 12. Aug. 25. Born Dec. 8, 1759. Unmarried Sister. Daughter of Dr. Adolph Meyer.
198. **Lewis Theophilus Mueller.** 1, r. xiii, 10. Aug. 25. Son of the Rev. George Godfrey Mueller. Aged one year.
199. **Susanna Caroline Lennert.** 1, l. xv, 5. May 17. Aged 9 months.

1804.

200. **Anna Elizabeth Frederick,** m.n. Freithardt. 1, l. xviii, 11. Jan. 7. Born in Rhenish Bavaria, 1719. Married, first, to Benjamin Nuss-

baum—two children, both dying at sea; and, secondly, to Abraham Frederlck, miller,—twelve children. Her oldest son, Abraham, lost his life in the Revolutionary War.

201. **Mary Penry.** 1, l. ix, 1. May 17. Unmarried Sister. She was born in Abergavenny, Wales, Nov. 12, 1735, the only daughter of Hughgonius and Mary (Stocker) Penry. Her father was a distinguished surgeon, but an improvident man; consequently, his wife, after his death, finding herself in straitened circumstances, gladly accepted an invitation from her married sister to come to Philadelphia and have a home with her. There the rough behavior of Mary's uncle (Atwood, a merchant, an unprincipled man) caused her much unhappiness; so that, after she had been spiritually awakened by the preaching of Brother Rogers, and told about Bethlehem and its Sisters' House by Valentine Haidt, the artist, she went there, in 1756, and joined that Sisterhood. In 1762 she came to live in the Lititz Sisters' House, and here, secure in God's love and the affection of her "choir" and the congregation, she served on the staff of her *Pflegerin* faithfully to the close of her life as the *"Schreiber"*— writer of the diary, copyist, book-keeper and secretary. She was also the *"Fremden-dienerin"* (visitors' guide), making in that capacity likewise many friends—among them those fine gentlemen Drs. Brown and Allison, who were attached to the U. S. Military Hospital, here, in 1778, and who after their removal corresponded with her. She died of bronchitis.

202. **John Schetter.** 1, r. xiii, 11. Aug. 27. Aged 7 months.

203. **Maria Russmeyer,** m.n. Evans. 1, l. xvii, 11. Sept. 21. Born Aug. 15, 1721, in Philadelphia; a daughter of Peter and Mary (Moore) Evans, and wife of Rev. Albrecht Russmeyer (No. 169). She had four children, of whom Maria, wife of Christian Schropp, survived her. Died of an epidemic fever.

204. **Anna Christina Meder,** m.n. Weber. 1, l. xvi, 1. Sept. 29. She was born 1741, in Wittgenstein, Germany. Her first husband was the Rev. Samuel Angerman, a missionary in Barbadoes, W. I., where he died; her second husband the Rev. John Meder, also a missionary in Barbadoes, but at the time of her death the Principal of the Girls' School in Lititz, (Linden Hall Seminary). In her first marriage she had one son, John Samuel, and in the second, another son, Christian Frederick, both surviving her in England.

205. **Conrad Westhaefer.** 1, r. xx, 9. Oct. 25. Born Nov. 19, 1737, in Muddy Creek (properly Mode Creek), Pa. His parents were Valentine Westhaefer, farmer, and Christina, m.n. Sandritter. In 1764 he married Catharine Heil, and had eleven children. His daughter Catharine married Gottfried Sebastian Oppelt, missionary among the Indians; Conrad, Jr., and John Gottfried moved to Ohio; John Leonhard and Jacob to York County. The father was a wheelwright.

206. **Frederick Kreiter.** 1, r. xiii, 12. Nov. 5. Infant son of Peter Abraham Kreiter.

207. **John Becker,** (his family name was Knecht). 1, l. xix, 9. Dec. 7. Born 1722, in Eberbach, Palatinate. Married Margaret Grosh, and had two sons, one of whom, John Leonhard, in Northampton Co., survived him. By trade a baker, but, as successor to Jasper Payne, he was for a number of years the congregation storekeeper.

208. **Anna Maria Schropp,** m.n. Russmeyer. 1, l. xvi, 2. Dec. 29. She was born in Bethlehem, July 12, 1757. In 1793 she married Christian Schropp, organist and schoolmaster in Lititz, and one son, Christian Russmeyer Schropp, was born to them.

1805.

209. **John Christopher Koenig.** 1, r. xviii, 9. June 7. A wheelwright, living near Lititz. He was born, 1745, in Koemnitz, Lower Silesia. Married, 1793, the widow Margaret Mueller, m.n. Schuetler.

210. **Verona Kiesel,** m.n. Leithold. 1, l. xvi, 3. June 29. She was born 1730, in Switzerland. Wife of George Frederick Kiesel. She had four sons and five daughters; one of the latter married Rev. Paul Weiss, pastor in Schoeneck. Her son, Abraham Frederick, lived near Lititz.

211. **John Goepfert.** 1, r. xvii. 9. Oct. 18. He was born in Mount Joy Township, 1745. A linen-weaver. He married Elizabeth Etter, and had five children; Christina married Christian Frederick, carpenter, and Magdalena married Daniel Rickert, farmer.

212. **Susanna Kreiter.** 1, l. xv, 6. Dec. 15. Infant daughter of Michael Christian Kreiter.

1806.

213. **Jacob Ricksecker.** 1, r. xvi, 1. Jan. 9. He was born in Donegal, Pa., April 24, 1745, a son of Peter and Anna (Jung) Ricksecker. Father and son were farmers. In 1769 he married Elizabeth Frederick. They had eight children.

214. **Elizabeth Eichler,** m.n. Kuehl. 1, l. xvi, 4. March 9. She was born April 4, 1763. Wife of Gottlieb Eichler, tobacconist. Four children survived her: Rachel, John Jacob, Abraham and John David.

215. **Anna Rosina Schenk.** 1, l. ix, 2. March 10. Unmarried Sister. Born in Lancaster, 1770.

216. **Claus Coelln.** 1, r. xvi, 2. April 6. Born, 1724, in Neuendorf, Holstein. United with the Moravians in Herrnhut, where he learned his trade of carpentry. Came to America in 1754, and after living two years in Nazareth, where he assisted in the building of Nazareth Hall, was sent to Lititz, and here he staid for the remainder of his life. In 1768 he married Elizabeth Lack, with whom he had five children: Anna Bernhardina (Harry), Gottlieb, John (who moved to York), Henry Renatus, a sailor, and Christian David, in the neighborhood. He was the master-carpenter who built the Brethren's and Sisters' Houses, the *Gemeinhaus* (present parsonage), the church, and nearly all of the houses in early Lititz; a fact to which he pointed, in his old age, with pardonable pride. For a few years he had charge of the congregation mill.

217. **Niels Tillofson.** 1, r. xvi, 3. April 15. He was born Feb. 4, 1745, in Holstein. After serving as a teacher in the Niesky Boys' School, and as the Superintendent of the Single Brethren in Gracehill, Ireland, he came, in 1791, to this country, and was ordained a Deacon of the Church by Bishop Ettwein. He married Hannah Warner; they had no children. Labored in the Gospel in Shoeneck, Gnadenhuetten on the Mahony, and was the Warden at Nazareth. Served also in Hope, N. J., but there he had the misfortune to fall into the drink habit, which, in addition to his self-imposed incompetency, gave offence to the congregation; therefore he was sent in retirement to Lititz, where, according to his pastor, Bishop Herbst, he did all he could to atone by repentant prayer and ever ready helpfulness for his past shame; and the same authority tells us that he had the love, or good-will, of every one.

218. **Francis Boehler.** 1, r. xvi, 4. June 4. He was born in Frankfort-on-the-Main, Sept., 1722. His parents were John Conrad and Elizabeth Antoinette (Hauf) Boehler. His first wife was Anna Catharine Jag, who died at Oldman's Creek, N. J., 1784. A second marriage was with the widow Anna (Rose) Unger. Two children died in their infancy. He was a retired minister, and died here while on a visit from Bethlehem.

219. **Maria Barbara Tshudy.** 1, l. xv, 7. Sept. 28. A daughter of Matthias Tshudy, aged 5 years.

220. **Catharine Kreiter.** 1, l. xvi, 5. Oct. 19. She was born in Oley, Pa., 1757. Her parents were Frederick and Elizabeth (Frey) Leinbach, and she was the wife of Frederick Peter Kreiter, cooper. Of her five children Samuel, born 1790, Susanna, 1794, and Daniel, 1799, survived her.

221. **Maria Paulick,** m.n. Bauermann. 1, l. xvi, 6. Nov. 5. With her is buried her still-born daughter. She was born in 1784, and was the wife of John George Paulick, blacksmith.

222. **Mary Magdalena Clewell.** 1, l. ix, 3. Dec. 20. Unmarried Sister. Born in Oley, 1745. She was a daughter of Francis Clewell, a farmer, who lived near Nazareth.

223. **Johanna Salome Schober.** 1, l. ix, 4. April 13. Unmarried Sister. She was born in 1772, a daughter of Andrew and Rosina (Thomas) Schober.

1807.

224. **John Henry Walther.** 1, r. ix, 2. Sept. 1. Unmarried. Born in Wackenheim, Palatinate, 1728.

225. **Barbara Blickensderfer,** m.n. Leuthold. 1, l. xvi, 7. Sept. 16. She was born in Switzerland, Aug. 8, 1740. She was the second wife of Christian Blickensderfer, Sr. No children.

226. **Henrietta Schoenlein.** 1, l. xv, 8. Dec. 1. Aged 2 months.

227. **Joseph Kreiter.** 1, r. xiii, 13. Dec. 5. Aged 3 months.

1808.

228. **Mary Rosina Mueller,** m.n. Unger. 1, l. xvi, 8. Feb. 24. She was born in Lancaster, April 27, 1775. Her parents were the Rev.

Frederick and Anna (Rose) Unger (later the second wife of Rev. Francis Boehler). Her husband was the Rev. John Constantine Mueller. No children. A fine soprano singer.

229. **Anna Margaret Kreiter.** 1, l. xvi, 9. March 1. She was born near Lancaster in 1736. Her maiden name was Hochstetter. Wife of John Kreiter. Of their ten children, Susanna Elizabeth was the third wife of Henry Van Vleck, hatter; Michael Christian and Peter Abraham lived near Lititz; Susanna Salome married the Rev. John Molther, and Maria Rosina was the wife of Christian Clewell of Shoeneck.

230. **Elizabeth Ricksecker,** m.n. Frederick. 1, l. xvi, 10. March 3. Born Nov. 9, 1747. Wife of Jacob Ricksecker, farmer near Lititz.

231. **Leonhard Schoenlein.** 1, r. xvi, 5. April 3. He was born in Linnelbach, Earldom of Wertheim, April 17, 1746. Married Margaret Fertig. Of their five children, Anna Regina, born in 1775, married Samuel Grosh, merchant, and John (1783) was, like his father, a weaver in Lititz.

232. **Verona Rudy,** m.n. Schnell. 1, l. xvi, 11. April 19. Born in 1722. Wife of Henry Rudy.

233. **Margaret Schoenlein,** m.n. Fertig. 1, l. iv, 1. June 13. Born March 1752, a daughter of John Christopher Fertig, the congregation's farmer. Wife of Leonhard Schoenlein.

234. **Christian Frederick Steinman.** 1, r. xvi, 6. June 17. He was born Nov. 8, 1739, in Epstein, near Manheim, in the Palatinate. Of Mennonite parentage, he united, in his sixteenth year, with the Moravians in Ebersdorf. Having come to this country, he was employed at Christiansprings on the farm and in the distillery, and after his marriage, in 1785, to Mary Magdalena Peitzel, he served for seven years as the Warden at Gnadenthal. After living for a number of years in Shoeneck, unofficially, but helping that congregation by word and deed, he and his wife came (April 13) to spend the remainder of their lives in Lititz. He was not related to the first Christian Frederick Steinman.

235. **John Grosh.** 1, r. xvi, 7. July 1. A son of John Valentine Grosh, born Feb. 2, 1734, in the Palatinate. His first wife was Barbara Bort, who died in 1781; then he married the widow Margaret Schenck (Fried), and after her death in 1795, the widow Mary Jansen (Fisher). By his first marriage he had six children, of whom Mary Magdalena, born 1765, married, first, Michael Kreiter, shoemaker, in Lititz, and secondly the Rev. John Martin Beck; Elizabeth, wife of John Christ, tinker, in Nazareth; Daniel, in Hempfield Township, and John Jacob, in Waterford on the Susquehanna.

236. **Anna Barbara Rank,** (m.n. Stauffer). 1, l. iv, 2. Aug. 1. Born in Warwick, 1738. Wife of Philip Rank, farmer. She had nine children, of whom John Philip, only, lived in this vicinity.

237. **Benjamin Lennert.** 1, r. xv, 1. Aug. 5. Aged one month.

238. **Elizabeth Hopson.** I, l. ix, 5. Oct. 12. Unmarried Sister. She was the daughter of John Hopson, Esq., a merchant and distinguished citizen of Lancaster. Her age was nearly fifty-two years.

239. **Henry Van Vleck.** I, r. xvi, 8. Oct. 21. Born Jan. 25, 1754, in New York, where his father, Henry Van Vleck, was a merchant. His mother's maiden name was Jane Cargill. In 1779 he married Maria Schmidt; in 1782, Elizabeth Riem, whose children were Abraham, born in 1784, and Sarah, who died in infancy. His third wife was Susanna Elizabeth Kreiter, with whom he had three children; Timotheus (died of small-pox), Isaac Renatus and Maria Henrietta. He was a hatter by trade, and an accomplished musician. In the afternoon of October 21 he went to the church to play in the Festival Lovefeast of the Larger Boys, and there, while in the act of tuning his violin, he fell from his seat unconscious to the floor—a preliminary of his death two hours later.

240. **John Schweishaupt.** I, r. xvi, 9. Nov. 15. He was born in Wendestein, Franconia, Feb. 11, 1721. Left an orphan at an early age, he was cared for by his godfather and taught the stocking-weaving trade. In 1745 he united with the Moravians in Herrnhaag, and when that settlement was abandoned came to Pennsylvania. In 1757 he married Anna Magdalena Rettenberger, and had two sons and a daughter who survived him. He was ordained a Deacon of the Church at Lancaster in 1762. Labored in the Gospel in Emmaus, Bethel, Warwick, Lancaster, York, Graceham, and in Donegal three times, in all 21 years. In his retirement, here, he found much pleasure in frequent visits to our country neighbors.

1809.

241. **Anna Elizabeth Weller.** I, l. ix, 6. Feb. 4. Unmarried Sister. Born near Graceham, Md., 1774. Her parents were John and Barbara (Krieger) Weller.

242. **Matthew Blickensderfer.** I, r. xx, 10. April 23. Born April 30, 1764, a son of Christian Blickensderfer, Sr. In 1789 he married Barbara Kichler; they had four children: Jacob, born 1790, Benjamin, 1792, William, 1795, and Rosina, 1800. His second marriage to Catharine Romig resulted in three children: Joshua, 1802, Matilda, 1806, and Henry, 1808. A farmer.

243. **Levi Phillips.** I, r. xv, 2 . Dec. 11. Aged 4 weeks.

1810.

244. **Ellert Coordsen.** I, r. xix, 10. March 1. Born in Holstein, July 9, 1724. United with the Brethren in Amsterdam and in 1756 came to this country. Married Anna Tanneberger. Served as a teacher in Moravian Boys' Schools abroad, and here, at Nazareth Hall and Emmaus, thirty-seven years. Was pastor at Schoeneck seven years. His final station was Heidelberg, Pa. Ordained a Deacon of the Church in 1792.

245. **Anna Magdalena Schweishaupt.** I, l. iv, 3. May 15. Born 1724 in Bergen, Hanover. Wife of Rev. John Schweishaupt. Her children

were John, who lived in Bethlehem; Magdalena, in Bethlehem, and Joseph, in Nazareth.

246. **Beata Lennert.** 1, l. xv, 9. July 2.

247. **Anna Johanna Masslich,** m.n. Gutjahr. 1, l. iv, 4. Sept. 1. Born 1755 in Lancaster. Wife of Gottlieb Masslich. Her children were John Ignatius, John Gottfried and Timothy.

248. **Emmanuel Kreiter.** 1, r. xiii, 14. Nov. 23. Born and died on the same day.

1811.

249. **Immanuel Bernhard Grosh.** 1, r. xv, 3. July 6. Born Dec. 13, 1806, a son of John Daniel and Margaret (Mies) Grosh.

250. **Leonhard Schoenlein.** 1, r. xv. 4. Born and died Aug. 16.

251. **Maria Salome Thomas (Gorner).** 1, l. iv, 5. Sept. 26. Born 1730 in Hornbach, Rhenish Bavaria. Wife of John Thomas, baker.

252. **Gottlieb Masslich.** 1, r. xviii, 10. Nov. 8. Born 1752 in Oderwitz, Upper Lusatia. Married Anna Johanna Gutjahr. His second wife was Justina Protzman.

253. **Louise Ann Blickensderfer.** 1, l. xv, 10. Dec. 21. Aged one year and seven months. Daughter of John Blickensderfer.

1812.

254. **Francis Jacob Ricksecker.** 1, r. xv, 5. Dec. 21. Infant.

255. **Philip Grosh.** 1, r. xvii, 10. Feb. 24. Shoemaker and farmer in Hempfield Township. Born 1732 in Eichloch, Palatinate, a son of John Valentine Grosh. Married Anna Margaret Rank. Their children were Matthew, John, Samuel, (born 1768), Maria, Christian, Peter (1774), Rosina, Michael, and George.

256. **Theodore Ferdinand Rauch.** 1, r. xv, 6. May 27. Infant son of Henry Gottfried Rauch.

257. **John George Kapp.** 1, r. xvi, 10. June 17. Born, 1740, in Upper Heidelberg Township. Married Anna Maria Kortz. No children.

258. **Joseph Hall.** 1, r. xv, 7. July 23. Infant son of Christian Hall.

259. **Sybilla Traeger.** 1, l. xv, 11. Aug. 24. Daughter of John Gottfried and Elizabeth (Hall) Traeger. Aged 9 years.

260. **Anna Maria Kreiter (Kohn).** 1, l. iv, 6. Oct. 30. Born in Bethlehem, 1745. Second wife of Peter Kreiter.

1813.

261. **Mary Magdalena Gladt.** 1, l. ix, 7. Jan. 8. Unmarried Sister. Born in Heidelberg, Pa., 1757. Consumption.

262. **Augusta Elizabeth Schoenlein.** 1, l. xv, 12. Feb. 5. Infant.

263. **Lewis Henry Benade.** 1, r. xv, 8. March 4. Aged 15 weeks. Son of the Rev. Andrew Benade.

264. **Benjamin Lichtenthaeler.** 1, r. xv, 9. Aged 11 days.

265. **Sarah Westhaeffer.** 1, l. ix, 8. May 24. Unmarried Sister. Born near Lititz, 1788, a daughter of Conrad Westhaefer, wheelwright.

266. **John Ricksecker.** 1, r. iv, 1. June 22. Born in Donegal, Pa., Jan. 3, 1749. Shoemaker. A son of Peter Ricksecker. Married Rachel

Frederick. Of their ten children John Jacob, born in 1779, lived in Shoeneck; John, 1789, and Frederick, 1792, in Lititz.

267. **Maria Elizabeth Petersen,** m.n. Rudy. 1, l. iv, 7. July 28. Born in Warwick, Oct. 23, 1779. Daughter of Heinrich Gottlob Rudy, and wife of Hans Petersen, baker. Two children.

268. **Elsa Catharine Petersen.** 1, l. xv, 13. Aug. 3. Aged 2 weeks. Daughter of the foregoing.

269. **Maria Susanna Levering.** 1, l. ix, 9. Sept. 22. Unmarried Sister. Born in Bethlehem, Feb. 24, 1794, a daughter of Rev. Abraham and Anna Christina (Cassler) Levering.

1814.

270. **Anna Catharina Westhaeffer,** m.n. Heil. 1, l. iv, 8. Feb. 4. Born in Warwick, Dec. 22, 1744, a daughter of Jacob and Catharine (Ruehl) Heil. Wife of Conrad Westhaeffer.

271. **Mary Magdalena Beck,** m.n. Grosh. 1, l. iv, 9. Feb. 16. Born Feb. 27, 1765, in Hempfield Township, a daughter of John Grosh. In 1785 she married Michael Gottfried Kreiter, with whom she had five children, one of whom was Jacob Kreiter (Greider), shoemaker, in Lititz. In 1810 she married the Rev. John Martin Beck. Intimately known as a midwife.

272. **William Lanius.** 1, r. iv, 2. March 11. Born in Hallam Township, six miles hitherward from York, Oct. 2, 1748, of parents associated with the Moravians. In his fourteenth year he was at Christianspring where he learned the tailor's trade, and in 1769 he married Elizabeth Heckedorn. They had no children. In 1789 he was called to Lititz to take charge of the congregation inn and served as its landlord satisfactorily for fourteen years. He was also the *"Fremden-diener"* (visitors' guide), and as such was missed and thankfully remembered, especially by the Principal of the Girls' School. He was a son of Jacob and Juliana (Kraemer) Lanius.

273. **Rosina Shober,** m.n. Thomas. 1, l. iv, 10. March 21. Born in Lancaster, 1750, a daughter of John and Salome (Gorner) Thomas. Came with her parents to Lititz in 1759. Married in 1769 Andrew Shober; he died in 1805, not at that time connected with the Church. Of her nine children she was survived by three sons and two daughters.

274. **John Jeter Miller.** 1, r. iv, 3. April 10. Born in Lehigh Township, Northampton Co., 1784. Married Susanna Mentzer, and had five children.

275. **Beatus Shoenlein.** 1, r. xv, 10. June 19.

1815.

276. **Anna Maria Christ,** m.n. Kleinmann. 1, l. iv, 11. Feb. 3. Born in Graceham, Md., 1759. Wife of Daniel Christ.

277. **Edwin Demetrius Bachman.** 1, r. xv, 11. March 31. Aged 10 months.

278. **Samuel Rank.** 1, r. iv, 4. May 22. He was born in Earl Township, July 30, 1742. Married Maria Salome Wordan, 1765. Of his five

children by this marriage, Anna Maria, Elizabeth and John survived
him. His second wife (m.n. Anna Margaret Kleinmann) bore him
two sons, Samuel and Peter.

279. **Mary Magdalena Chitty.** 1, l. ix, 10. Oct. 14. Unmarried Sister.
Born in Hope, N. C., July 16, 1787, a daughter of Benjamin Chitty.

280. **Daniel Christ.** 1, r. iv, 5. Nov. 23. Born 1744, near Manheim, in
the Palatinate, a son of Christian and Maria Catharine (Berchtol)
Christ. By trade a linen-weaver. His first wife was Eva Barbara
Grosh. Of their five children, Christian was settled in Lititz; Maria
Catharine married Jacob Blum, merchant, Salem, N. C., and Susanna
Magdalena married Jacob Rock, tailor, in Lititz. In 1790 he married
Anna Maria Kleinmann. Of her five children, Julianna, born 1791,
married Jacob Greider, shoemaker; and Anna Sophia and Matthew
also lived, at that time, in Lititz. He played the French-horn and
alto-trombone in the church music.

281. **Philip Rank.** 1, r. iv, 6. Nov. 25. A son of John Michael and Anna
Barbara Rank, he was born in Earl Township, Jan. 30, 1734. Married Anna Barbara Stauffer, and had nine children. John Michael
moved to Ohio; Anna Barbara married Jacob Schnall, farmer in
Old Nazareth; Anna Maria married the Rev. John Peter Kluge.

282. **Christina Frederick,** m.n. Goepfert. 1, l. iv, 12. Dec. 8. Born in
Donegal, Pa., 1777. Wife of Christian Frederick. Four children.

283. **Maria Elizabeth Rauch,** m.n. Kiesel. 1, l. iv, 13. Dec. 30. Born at
Muddy Creek, Pa., 1738. Her first husband was Henry Xander;
her second, Henry Romig, with whom she had five sons and two
daughters; her third was John Henry Rauch.

1816.

284. **Christine Ronner,** m.n. Michael. 1, l. iv, 14. Jan. 19. Born 1741, in
the Palatinate. Wife of Anton Ronner, tailor, who died in 1799.
Two children; both died in infancy.

285. **Christian Goodyear (Gutjahr).** 1, r. iv, 7. Feb. 29. Born in Lancaster, 1746, and in 1759 came with his parents John Christian and
Margaret (Roesner) Gutjahr to the neighborhood of Lititz. Married Charlotte Jungblut. They had eight children. In the course of
time he moved into Lititz, and here he had charge of the Brethren's
House farm.

286. **Maria Sophia Reinke.** 1, l. iii, 1. April 19. She was born in
Eristfer, Livonia, April 20, 1755. Her parents were the Rev. John
Henry Rudolph and Anna, David Schneider's oldest daughter, of
Zauchtenthal. In 1783 she was married to the Rev. Carl Gottlieb
Reichelt and went with him to St. Thomas, where he died. She had
one daughter (posthumous) by this marriage. In 1786 she became
the wife of Abraham Reinke, Jr. They had three sons and three
daughters.

287. **Maria Grosh,** m.n. Fischer. 1, l. iii, 2. June 3. Born in Würtemberg, 1737. Wife of John Grosh.

288. **Charlotte Goodyear** (Gutjahr), m.n. Jungblut. 1, l. iii, 3. Oct. 12.
Born near Lititz, 1759. Wife of Christian Goodyear. Eight children.
289. **Peter Regennas.** 1, r. xv, 12. Oct. 20. Infant.
290. **Elizabeth Rank.** 1, l. ix, 11. Dec. 22. Unmarried Sister. Born in
1770, a daughter of Samuel and Maria Salome (Worden) Rank.

1817.

291. **Charles William Shoenlein.** 1, r. xv, 13. Jan. 21. Aged 3 months.
292. **John David Petersen.** 1, r. viii, 1. March 15. Aged 5 years.
293. **Catharine Protzman.** 1, l. viii, 1. April 28. Unmarried Sister. Born
in Maryland, May 28, 1756.
294. **Joseph Sturgis.** 1, r. iv, 8. June 9. Born in Philadelphia, a son of
Joseph Sturgis (English), March 16, 1738, and baptized by Whitefield. His mother's maiden name was Jane Hatfield; she and her
sons Cornelius and Joseph were Moravian church-members. A
pupil in the Boys' School at Germantown, he moved with that institution successively to Oley, to Macungie, and to Bethlehem. As a
lad of sixteen he was sent to Gnadenhuetten on the Mahony to as-
sist there in the household; and on the night of Nov. 24, 1755, when
its Mission-house was burned and eleven Brethren and Sisters were
massacred, he was one of the few that escaped. He rushed for
safety to the roof, found it in flames, and then jumped from a garret
window to the ground and fled to the forest; twice, in quick suc-
cession, fired upon by the savages—one bullet grazing his chin and
another more seriously the top of his head. In 1766 he married
Margaret Stoehr, and lived in Lebanon, following his trade—that
of potter—until, in 1782, he moved to Lititz. From 1803 to 1811
they lived in York, and then returned to Lititz to the care of his son
Samuel. He had seven sons and three daughters; thirty-four grand
and three great-grandchildren.
295. **Mary Magdalena Steinman,** m.n. Peitzel. 1, l. iii, 4. Nov. 1. She
was born in York, Dec. 14, 1745. Wife of Christian Frederick
Steinman (second).
296. **John Phillips.** 1, r. iv, 9. Nov. 2. Born in Northampton Co., in
1769. Married Wilhelmina Rosina Gutman; nine children. A
tailor. He served many years as Chief-Sacristan; also as Visitors'
Guide.
297. **Anna Christina Cassler,** m.n. Goettel. 1, l. iii, 5. Nov. 12. Born in
Seligen, Rhenish Bavaria, Nov. 14, 1726. Wife of William Cassler;
ten children; four sons and six daughters.

1818.

298. **John George Geitner,** (second). 1, r. iv, 10. Feb. 28. Born in Bethlehem, July 29, 1760. A tanner. Married Maria Elizabeth Kreiter;
five children; one son, Jacob, and four daughters.
299. **Elizabeth Oehme,** m.n. Frevel. 1, l. iii, 6. May 5. Born in the
vicinity of Philadelphia, Feb. 22, 1761. Wife of John Erdman
Oehme; three sons and three daughters.

300. **Henry Gottlob Rudy.** i, r. iv, 11. May 8. Born in Warwick, 1750, a son of Henry and Verona (Schnell) Rudy. He married Maria Elizabeth Merck. They had eight children,—two sons and six daughters. In the congregation he was the chief *"diener"* (sacristan), coming faithfully, in rain and shine, from his farm, three miles away, to attend to that duty.

301. **Anna Margaretha Grosh (Rank).** i, l. iii, 7. Born in Earl Township, 1740, a daughter of John Michael Rank. Wife of Philip Grosh. Seven sons and two daughters.

302. **John Gottfried Masslich.** i, r. ix, 3. Nov. 21. Unmarried. Born, 1798. Son of Gottlieb Masslich.

1819.

303. **Maria Salome Kreiter,** m.n. Borroway. i, l. iii, 8. Jan. 6. Born in Donegal, 1762. Wife of Christian Andrew Kreiter.

304. **Anna Catharine Schnall,** m.n. Goepfert. i, l. iii, 9. Feb. 2. Born near Mount Joy, 1769. Daughter of John Goepfert, and wife of Thomas Schnall.

305. **Carl Uria Oehme.** i, r. viii, 2. Feb. 12. Born 1807, a son of John Erdman Oehme.

306. **Peter Abraham Kreiter.** i, r. iv, 12. Feb. 13. Born March 17, 1771. A son of John and Anna Margaretha (Hochstetter) Kreiter. Married Maria Elizabeth Ricksecker. Four sons and three daughters.

307. **Maria Charlotte Sturgis.** i, l. vii, 1. Feb. 24. Aged 8 years. Daughter of Samuel Sturgis, potter.

308. **Samuel Steinke.** i, r. iii, 1. March 13. Born in Osterode, Prussia, 1743. Coppersmith. Married Elizabeth Busch. One son and three daughters.

309. **Polycarpus Kohn Kreiter.** i, r. viii, 3. March 17. Aged 9 months. Son of Benjamin Kreiter, nailsmith.

310. **Beata Rock.** i, l. vii, 2. March 18.

311. **Gottfried Heinrich Thumhardt.** i, r. iii, 2. June 13. He was born in Graefenrode, Thuringia, Aug. 27, 1745. Studied medicine in Gotha. United with the Brethren in Gnadau, 1775; and having married Theresa Schneider, 1776, in Herrnhut, they went as missionaries to St. Thomas, suffering direst shipwreck on the voyage thither. There he served, chiefly as a physician, until 1791, when, because of impaired health, he relinquished that calling and came to Pennsylvania, locating in Lititz. Here for twenty-six years, the congregation had the valued benefit of his medical knowledge.

312. **Benjamin Rudolphi.** i, r. viii, 4. Aug. 4. Aged one year. Son of Dr. Rudolphi.

1820.

313. **Anna Maria Tannenberg,** m.n. Fischer. i, l. iii, 10. April 19. Born in Heidelberg, Pa., Feb. 2, 1743. She was thrice married: in 1772 to James Hall, in 1785 to Gottlieb Lange, and in 1800 to David Tannenberg, organ-builder. In her first marriage she had three sons and one daughter.

314. **Orlando Washington Eichler.** i, r. viii, 5. Sept. 6. Aged 10 mos.

1821.

315. **Margaretha Sturgis,** m.n. Stoehr. 1, l. iii, 11. March 1. Born in Lancaster Co., 1740. Wife of Joseph Sturgis.

316. **George Gottfried Mueller.** 1, r. iii, 3. March 19. Presbyter. He was born in Gross Hennersdorf, Upper Lusatia, May 22, 1762. He married Anna Johanna Levering; they had three children. Was pastor of various Moravian congregations. Visited David Zeisberger on his death-bed, and preached the German sermon at his funeral. Especially proficient as a violinist, he led the orchestra in the Lititz Brethren's House during his stay there as its *Pfleger.* "Brother Mueller was quickly recalled from Lancaster because a certain Herr (John) Randolph, Ex-Governor of Virginia and now Attorney-General of the United States, who came here yesterday evening, on his way to Philadelphia, to visit us, wished to hear our music." (Brethren's House Diary, May 30, 1791.) In his last years he served as Superintendent of the Married Members in the Lititz congregation. Died of consumption.

317. **Carl Frederick Shroeter.** 1, r. iii, 4. March 28. Deacon of the Church; formerly a missionary in Surinam; retired in Lititz. Born in Seehausen, Brandenburg, Oct. 31, 1750. United with the Brethren in Gnadau. Married Anna Catharina Stiefel of Herrnhut. In 1799 he was the Superintendent of the Single Brethren in Salem, N. C.

318. **Anna Maria Maehr,** m.n. Tshudy. 1, l. iii, 12. June 21. Born April 6, 1764, a daughter of Christian and Eva Barbara (Kiesel) Tshudy. In 1799 she married the Rev. John Frederick Metz, missionary, who died in Paramaribo. Her second marriage was to the Rev. John Maehr, also a missionary in South America.

319. **Miriam Traeger.** 1, l. vii, 3. Aug. 3. Aged five months.

320. **Jacob Shoenlein.** 1, r. viii, 6. Sept. 11. Aged one day.

321. **Gottlieb Eichler.** 1, r. iii, 5. Sept. 26. Born in Lower Oderwitz, Upper Lusatia, Aug. 14, 1758. His first wife was Benigna Klotz, of Lititz. Louisa was their only child. In 1791 he married Elizabeth Kiehl; they had four children. His third wife was Elizabeth Frevel, of Nazareth. By trade, a tobacconist.

322. **Elizabeth Goepfert,** m.n. Etter. 1, l. iii, 13. Oct. 6. Born in Donegal, Pa., 1747. Wife of John Goepfert. Five children.

323. **John Abraham Ricksecker.** 1, r. iii, 6. Oct. 18. Born in Lititz, 1788, a son of Jacob Ricksecker, farmer. Died while on a visit here from his home in Gnadenhuetten, Ohio. Married Maria Blickensderfer. Of four children, two survived him.

324. **Matilda Louisa Rudolphi.** 1, l. vii, 4. Nov. 4. Aged 16 days.

325. **Lavinia Theresa Christ.** 1, l. vii, 5. Nov. 12. Daughter of Christian Christ. Aged three years.

1822.

326. **John George Geitner,** third. 1, r. viii, 7. Jan. 4. A son of Jacob Geitner, aged five months.

327. **Charles Lichtenthaeler.** 1, r. viii, 8. Jan. 17. One year old.

328. **Anna Nielsen.** 1, l. viii, 2. Jan. 22. Unmarried Sister. Born in Nazareth, 1745.

329. **Augusta Charlotte Rock.** 1, l. vii, 6. April 10. Daughter of Jacob Rock, aged five years.

330. **Henry Godfrey Rauch.** 1, r. iii, 7. April 22. A son of John Henry and Catharine (Goodyear) Rauch, born in Lititz, July 13, 1781. Married Rosina Kornman; three children.

331. **John David Eichler.** 1, r. ix, 4. April 26. Unmarried. A son of Gottlob Eichler, born in Lititz, Oct. 1800.

332. **Margaret Georgiana Levering,** m.n. Jones. 1, l. iii, 14. April 28. Born in Myford, North Wales, June 3, 1796. Wife of John Levering.

333. **Maria Henrietta Van Vleck.** 1, l. viii, 3. May 5. Unmarried Sister. Born in Lititz, 1797, a daughter of Henry and Susanna Elizabeth (Kreiter) Van Vleck. Died of consumption.

334. **Benjamin Chitty.** 1, r. iii, 8. July 12. Born in Frederick Co., Md., March 14, 1743, a son of Benjamin and Sarah (Palmer) Chitty. He was a half-brother of Mary Tippet (400) and Catharine Toon (60). In 1765 he married Mary Padget. Of their ten children Elizabeth was married to the Rev. Nathanael Braun, Dorcas to David Peter, and Sarah to Samuel Luckenbach.

335. **Daniel Henry Christ.** 1, r. viii, 9. July 12. Aged 2 years.

1823.

336. **Maria Henrietta Kreiter.** 1, l. vii, 7. Aged five weeks. Daughter of Michael Kreiter, landlord of Lititz Inn.

337. **Juliana Geitner.** 1, l. vii, 8. March 29. Aged 8 weeks.

338. **John Henry Shoenlein.** 1, r. viii, 10. April 17. Infant.

339. **Charlotte Wilhelmina (Lembke) Eberman.** 1, l. xx, 12. April 25. Born May 28, 1793, in Graceham, Md. Her parents were Christian William and Anna Maria (Demuth) Lembke. Married the Rev. William Eberman, 1819. She had two children, of whom Francis survived her.

340. **Elizabeth Romania Rudy.** 1, l. vii, 9. July 14. Aged one year.

341. **Catharine Muecke,** m.n. Blickensderfer. 1, l. xix, 12. Aug. 30. Born in Lititz, May 17, 1761, a daughter of Christian and Catharine (Sherger) Blickensderfer. Married Matthew Muecke, 1782, and had seven sons and one daughter.

342. **Anna Maria Kiesel.** 1, l. viii, 4. Sept. 27. Unmarried Sister. Born at Kiesel-hill, near Lititz, 1774. Daughter of Frederick Kiesel.

343. **George Hoeffer.** 1, r. ix, 5. Oct. 4. Unmarried. Born in Lancaster, 1795.

344. **George Henry Frederick.** 1, r. vii, 1. Oct. 7. Aged three years.

345. **Charles Miller.** 1, r. ix, 6. Oct. 9. Born Jan. 8, 1809, a son of Peter Miller.

346. **William Adolph Grosh.** 1, r. vii, 2. Oct. 11. Aged 19 months. A son of Peter Grosh.

347. **Julius Cunow Bechler.** i, r. vii, 3. Oct. 18. Born in Nazareth Hall, Feb. 7, 1819; a son of the Rev. John C. Bechler, pastor and Principal of the Girls' School in Lititz.

348. **William Lennert Seaber.** i, r. vii, 4. Oct. 31. Born in Warwick, 1812, a son of Jacob Seaber.

349. **Delia Belinda Shoenlein.** i, l. vii, 10. Aged four years.

1824.

350. **Christian Andrew Kreiter.** i, r. xx, 11. Jan. 4. Born in Hempfield Township, July 11, 1751. His parents were Peter and Maria (Hirschy) Kreiter. In 1784 he married Regina Fertig, who died in 1786. His second wife (1801) was Maria Salome Borroway. No children in either marriage.

351. **Edward Levering Kreiter.** i, r. viii, 11. Jan. 16. Infant son of Michael and Anna (Levering) Kreiter.

352. **Beatus Rickert.** i, r. vii, 5. March 14.

353. **Magdalena Rickert,** m.n. Goepfert. i, l. xviii, 12. March 21. Born in Rapho Township, Lancaster Co., Dec. 26, 1782. Wife of Daniel Rickert.

354. **Beatus Rudy.** i, r. vii, 6. March 26.

355. **John Gottfried Traeger.** i, r. iii, 9. May 31. Born in Friedersdorf, Upper Lusatia, Nov. 3, 1769. Married Elizabeth Hall, 1800. Ten children. He was a useful man, esteemed as a leader in the councils of his church. By trade a shoemaker.

356. **Johanna Carolina Levering,** m.n. Schnall. i, l. iii, 15. July 31. She was born in Gnadenthal, near Nazareth, July 15, 1800, a daughter of the Rev. John Schnall, missionary in New Fairfield, Canada. In 1823, she married the widower John Levering, merchant, in Lititz, and died one hour after the birth of her first child, a daughter.

357. **Anna Maria Werner,** m.n. Kiesel. i, l. xvii, 12. Aug. 7. Born at Muddy Creek, Pa., 1741. Wife of William Werner.

358. **Maria Amalia Harry.** i, l. viii, 5. Sept. 4. Unmarried Sister. Born in Lititz, 1799.

359. **Maria Sophia Beck.** i, l. vii, 11. Sept. 25. Born July 5, 1822, a daughter of John and Johanna Augusta (Reinke) Beck.

360. **Maria Cecilia Geitner.** i, l. vii, 12. Sept. 27. Aged 7 months..

361. **Caroline Sophia Bechler.** i, l. vii, 13. Oct. 1. A daughter of the Rev. John C. Bechler, Pastor in Lititz.

362. **Anna Maria Kreiter,** m.n. Seyfried. i, l. vii, 15. Oct. 16. Born in Friedensthal, near Nazareth, Sept. 15, 1784, a daughter of Nicholas Seyfried. She was the wife of Benjamin Kreiter, farmer and Justice of the Peace. Four sons and three daughters.

363. **Catharine Charlotte Sturgis.** i, l. xv, 14. Oct. 22. Aged 18 hours.

364. **Francis Lennert Kreiter.** i, r. vii, 7. Oct. 24. Aged eight weeks. A son of Daniel Kreiter, saddler.

365. **John Miller.** i, r. iii, 10. Oct. 29. Born in Lititz, 1794, a son of John Miller, dyer.

366. **Hans Petersen.** 1, r. iii, 11. Nov. 18. Born in Taustrup, Jutland, Dec. 4, 1764. His parents were Peter Hansen and Elizabeth, m.n. Peters. Served ten years in Denmark as a soldier. Came with Bro. Martin Hansen to this country in 1802. By trade a baker. In 1806 he married Maria Elizabeth Rudy, who died in 1813; their two children died in infancy. His second wife was Rachel Ricksecker, and their children were Lucinda Amelia, born 1816, Anna Eliza, 1818, Mary Anne, 1820, and Rebecca Catharine, 1823. Anna Eliza was married to the Rev. John Regennas.

367. **Maria Barbara Milchsack,** m.n. Regin. 1, l. xvi, 12. Nov. 27. Born in Lancaster, 1765. Wife of George Milchsack, who died in 1804. Five sons and five daughters.

1825.

368. **John Frederick Rudolphi.** 1, r. iii, 12. March 3. Born in Arneburg, Brandenburg, Oct. 19, 1763. Studied medicine and surgery. United with the Brethren in Herrnhut, 1783, and went in the same year as medical missionary to Tranquebar and on the Nicobar Islands, where he stayed six years and then returned to Herrnhut, practicing surgery there for two years. In 1795 he came to Bethlehem and served that congregation and its neighborhood as physician and surgeon, twenty years. In 1796 he married Sophia Magdalena Otto; seven children: in 1809, Anna Schaaf; no children: and in 1815 he married Elizabeth Frey, with whom he had three children. In 1816 he moved to Warwick, and in 1824 to Lititz, practicing his profession in both places.

369. **Ferdinand Lichtenthaeler.** 1, r. vii, 8. April 4. A son of Adolph Lichtenthaeler, aged two years.

370. **Josephine Matilda Sturgis.** 1, l. xv, 15. April 17. Infant daughter of Samuel Sturgis.

371. **George Siwelly Rogers.** 1, r. vii, 9. May 9. Infant son of John Jarvis Rogers, M.D.

372. **Barbara Rauch,** m.n. Rudy. 1, l. xx, 13. May 25. Born in Warwick, 1792, a daughter of Henry Rudy. Wife of John William Rauch. Four sons and one daughter.

373. **Beata Eberman.** 1, l. xiv, 14. June 21.

374. **Francis William Schmidt.** 1, r. vii, 10. Oct. 1. Infant.

1826.

375. **Maria Elizabeth Kreiter,** m.n. Ricksecker. 1, l. xix, 13. March 3. Born in Warwick, 1777. Wife of Peter Abraham Kreiter.

376. **John Peter Lennert.** 1, r. xix, 11. April 10. Born in Gnadenthal, near Nazareth, July 30, 1755. A tinsmith. His first wife was Elizabeth Baumgaertner; their daughter Rebecca married Christian Youngman. In 1797 he married Johanna Susanna Knauss. The Rev. William Lawrence Lennert was the third son of the second marriage.

4

377. **Emma Maria Augusta Reinke.** 1, l. xiv, 15. May 2. Born in Lancaster, 1820, a daughter of the Rev. Samuel Reinke, Principal of the Lititz Girls' School, and Susanna Theodora, m.n. Eyerle.

378. **Andrew James Ricksecker.** 1, r. vii, 11. Aug. 4. Two years old. A son of Frederick Ricksecker.

379. **Sarah Ann Cacy.** 1, l. viii, 6. Sept. 19. Born in Queen Anne Co., Eastern shore of Maryland, Dec. 24, 1811. A pupil in the Lititz Girls' School (Linden Hall), the first one to die there.

380. **Susanna Theodora Reinke,** m.n. Eyerle. 1, l. xviii, 13. Sept. 21. Born in Nazareth, Dec. 17, 1796. Daughter of Jacob Eyerle and Anna Maria, m.n. Frey. Wife of the Rev. Samuel Reinke.

381. **Lawrence Peter Kreiter.** 1, r. xv, 14. Nov. 27. Seven weeks old. Son of Daniel Kreiter.

382. **Michael Jung.** 1, r. ix, 7. Dec. 13. Unmarried. Born in Engoldsheim, Alsatia, Jan. 5, 1743. In his eighth year he came with his parents to Broadbay, Maine, and lived there until 1767, when he removed to Bethlehem. He served as a missionary among the Indians for twenty-eight years. Retired in Lititz, 1813.

383. **Christian Schropp.** 1, r. xviii, 11. Dec. 31. Born June 27, 1756, in Bethlehem, where his father, Matthew Schropp, was Warden of the congregation. His mother's maiden name was Maria Thomet. In 1793 he married Anna Maria Russmeyer; their son, Christian Russmeyer, died in 1821. His second wife (1806) was Rebecca Edmonds. He was by trade a nailsmith, but served the congregation for many years as its schoolmaster, and many there were who, in after years, cherished a kindly remembrance of him. A fine musician, he was of use to the church, musically, in various ways, but especially as its organist,—a position he held for forty years.

1827.

384. **Maria Elizabeth Rudy,** m.n. Merck. 1, l. xvii, 13. Feb. 6. Born in Lititz, 1758. Wife of Henry Gottlob Rudy.

385. **John Martin Beck.** 1, r. xvii, 11. Feb. 14. Born in Schafhausen, Switzerland, Sept. 29, 1746, the oldest son of Alexander Beck, *Stadt Musicus,* and Barbara, m.n. Schnetzler. Spiritually awakened by the preaching of Moravian itinerants in his native city, he united with the Brethren in Neuwied, and came to be a very successful teacher there in the Boys' School. In 1786 he received a call to America. On the voyage hither he made a providential escape—"a direct answer to the prayers of the Brethren on board"—from imminent death or slavery; for their vessel was chased by an Algerine pirate who had come so near them that the gleam of his crew's naked sabres could be seen and their blood-thirsty threats distinctly heard, when his ship was caught and whirled in a sudden squall, its rigging torn, and its progress hindered, leaving the Brethren's vessel to sail away in peace. Some of his fellow-voyagers—destined for Lititz—were John Herbst (later, Bishop), John Erdman Oehme, and Gottlieb Eichler, the latter also mentioning in his memoir the above occurrence. In Bethlehem he was again engaged in teaching boys, until, in 1790, he married Anna Johanna Grubé and went with her to his first ministry

in Emmaus, he having been previously ordained a Deacon of the Church by Bishop Huebner. Other pastorates of his were Graceham, Donegal, Bethel, Lancaster (twice) and York. His wife died in 1808. Their children were John, Benigna Louise, and Johanna Elizabeth. In 1812 he married Mary Magdalena Kreiter, m.n. Grosh, and with her served the Lititz congregation as Superintendents of the Married Members, he at the same time practicing medicine, in which he had considerable skill.

386. **Beatus Kreiter.** 1, r. xiv, 14. March 1.

1828.

387. **Beata Rauch.** 1, l. xiii, 15. March 30.
388. **Anna Maria Protzman,** m.n. Buehler. 1, l. xvi, 13. April 8. Born near Lititz, 1751. In 1772 was married to Peter Spiker, and at the time of her death her five sons and one daughter were living in Pittsburg and Ohio. In 1786 she was married to Daniel Protzman, of Graceham, Md.
389. **Jacob Abraham Cassler.** 1, r. xiii, 15. April 12. Seven months old.
390. **Anna Maria Geitner.** 1, l. xiii, 16. May 5. Aged seven months.
391. **Anna Maria Beck.** 1, l. viii, 7. May 16. Unmarried Sister. Born in Lebanon, Dec. 7, 1752, a daughter of Philip Beck. Lived in the Sisters' House, where she was blind for the last thirty-one years of her life, yet busy always with her spinning and knitting.
392. **Louise Pauline Muecke.** 1, l. xv, 16. May 22. Infant.
393. **Christian Christ.** 1, r. xvi, 11. June 19. Born in Lititz, Nov. 7, 1773, a son of Daniel and Barbara (Grosh) Christ. May 13, 1810, he married Anna Julianna Christ (a daughter of Peter Christ, tawer, who moved to Nazareth). He was survived by three children, Carolina Elizabeth, Peter Augustus and Francis William. He served the congregation many years in the Wardens' College and as chief *"Saal-diener."*
394. **Maria Rudy.** 1, l. xiv, 16. July 10. Lived one hour.

1829.

395. **Mary Anne Kaufman.** 1, l. viii, 8. Jan. 29. Born in East Hempfield Township, Jan. 25, 1814, a daughter of John Kaufman, landlord of the Lititz Inn. Her mother's maiden name was Becker.
396. **Henry Augustus Kummer.** 1, r. xv, 15. Feb. 27. Born Dec. 22, 1827, a son of the Rev. John Gottlob Kummer, Principal of the Lititz Girls' School (Linden Hall).
397. **Mary Anne Susanna Muecke.** 1, l. xiii, 17. March 19. Aged 9 months.
398. **Mary Magdalena Grosh.** 1, l. viii, 9. April 1. Born July 22, 1813. Her parents were Peter Grosh, farmer of one of the congregation farms, and Catharine, m.n. Conrad.
399. **Francis Eugene Bechler.** 1, r. ix, 8. April 15. Born on Staten Island, Dec. 7, 1815. A son of the Rev. John C. Bechler, Pastor in Lititz.

400. **Mary Tippet.** 1, 1. viii, 10. April 23. Unmarried Sister. She was born in Carroll's Manor, Md., April 11, 1750. Her mother's maiden name was Sarah Palmer. Received into the Lititz congregation and the Sisters' House in 1768. Her first charge there was of the larger girls. "The training of young people," she writes, was always, notwithstanding its difficulties, a pleasure to me." In 1784 she was appointed the *Pflegerin* of her "Choir;" in 1798 received a call from Bethlehem to serve there in the same capacity; and in 1809 was recalled to Lititz where she continued in the same service eight more years. After thirty-seven years of official life, she retired from active duty in 1817.

401. **William Cassler.** 1, r. xx, 12. May 6. Born in Philadelphia, July 15, 1754. Married Rosina, daughter of David Tannenberg, organbuilder. Of his children, William, Lewis David, Samuel, and John Christian survived him.

402. **Jacob Rauschenberger.** 1, r. xix, 12. Aug. 3. Born in Hope, N. J., 1779. A Deacon of the Church; late Pastor of the Gnadenhuetten, Ohio, congregation; retired in Lititz on account of ill-health. His wife was Margaret Huber. Formerly a teacher in Nazareth Hall.

403. **Elizabeth Shoenlein.** 1, 1. xx, 14. Sept. 18. Born in Lititz, 1786. Daughter of Jacob Ricksecker and wife of John Shoenlein. Ten children; survived only by Juliana and Joseph.

404. **John Michael Kraemer.** 1, r. xviii, 12. Nov. 22. Born in Lancaster, 1744. Son of Michael and Catharine Kraemer. Married Elizabeth Schneider. Ten children.

1830.

405. **Johanna Caroline Tshudy.** 1, 1. xix, 14. March 15. She was born in Lititz, Nov. 28, 1806, a daughter of the Rev. Abraham Levering, Warden of the congregation. First wife of Jacob Blickensderfer Tshudy.

406. **Daniel Florian Loudy.** 1, r. xvii, 12. May 23. Born in Neuwied, 1791. Came to Lititz in 1820, and married Anna Wilhelmina Kreiter. They lived in Warwick where he had his own weaver's shop. A superior French-horn player,—having been attached to a military band in Germany—he frequently accompanied our trombonists with his instrument, much to the delight of the congregation and somewhat to the chagrin of the resident players of brass. Died of small-pox.

407. **Elizabeth Albright.** 1, 1. xviii, 14. June 4. Born in Lebanon Co., Pa., Aug. 14, 1739, a daughter of Balthasar and Anna Catharina (Rhoemer) Orth. Wife of Andrew Albright.

408. **Barbara Miller,** m.n. Porter. 1, 1. xvii, 14. June 19. Born in Warwick, 1796. Daughter of Matthew Porter, of Lancaster, and wife of Jacob Miller.

409. **James Theodore Keller.** 1, r. xiv, 15. June 22. Aged 3 months.

410. **Francis Harry Muecke.** 1, r. xiii, 16. June 22. One month old.

411. **Ernst Julius Bachman.** 1, r. ix, 9. Aug. 24. Unmarried. School-master near Lebanon. Born in Nazareth, Oct. 18, 1801. Son of John Philip Bachman.
412. **Henry Levering Kreiter.** 1, r. xv, 16. Sept. 29. Aged six months.
413. **Thomas Daniel Kreiter.** 1, r. xiv, 16. Oct. 1. Infant son of Daniel and Maria Louisa (Lennert) Kreiter.
414. **Charles Henry Kiesel.** 1, r. xiii, 17. Oct. 21. Ten years old.

1831.

415. **Elizabeth Lanius,** m.n. Heckedorn. 1, l. xvi, 14. Jan. 12. Wife of William Lanius.
416. **Aaron Kreiter.** 1, r. vi, 1. Jan. 17. Three days old.
417. **Juliana Schott.** 1, l. xv, 17. Feb. 19. Infant.
418. **Anna Maria Miller (Frederick).** 1, l. xx, 15. Feb. 28. Born in Mount Joy Township, Nov. 28, 1760, a daughetr of Abraham Frederick. Wife of John Miller.
419. **Lewis Gustavus Hamm.** 1, r. vi, 2. March 12. Infant son of John and Louisa Hamm.
420. **George Henry Thomas.** 1, r. vi, 3. April 11. Infant son of John and Lydia (Frank) Thomas.
421. **Amelia Regina Lebolde Demuth.** 1, l. viii, 11. July 17. Un-married Sister. Born in Lancaster, 1808, a daughter of Jacob De-muth, tobacconist.
422. **Matilda Ferrel.** 1, l. ix, 12. Aug. 21. Unmarried Sister. Born near Reading, 1813. Daughter of Joseph and Catharine (Knauss) Ferrel.
423. **Elizabeth Feisser.** 1, l. viii, 12. Sept. 5. Unmarried Sister. Born in York, 1758; daughter of John and Elizabeth (Schlatter) Feisser.
424. **Catharina Grosh,** m.n. Matter. 1, l. xix, 15. Dec. 19. Born Nov. 10, 1808. Wife of Timothy Grosh.

1832.

425. **John Jacob Hamm.** 1, r. vi, 4. Feb. 12. Infant son of John and Louisa (Dinges) Hamm.
426. **John Cassler.** 1, r. ix, 10. March 14. Unmarried. Born June 18, 1811, near Lititz. Son of John Christian Cassler.
427. **Henry Frederick.** 1, r. vi, 5. March 20. Aged one year.
428. **Elizabeth Siess.** 1, l. xii, 13. March 25. Unmarried Sister. Born in Heidelberg, Pa., 1759. Daughter of John George and Maria (Dock) Siess.
429. **Catharine Fetter.** 1, l. ix, 13. April 10. Unmarried Sister. Born in Lancaster, 1766, a daughter of Gottlieb Fetter.
430. **Beata Blickensderfer.** 1, l. xvii, 17. May 5. Daughter of Henry and Elvina Blickensderfer.
431. **Lydia Muecke.** 1, l. xviii, 15. May 9. Born in Lititz, 1776. Daughter of Isaac Renatus Harry, and wife of Michael Muecke. Three children, of whom Sabina Emily was the oldest.
432. **John Fuehrer.** 1, r. xii, 12. May 17. Unmarried. Born in Old Nazareth, 1760.

433. **Ellen Eliza Ann Thomas.** 1, l. xiii, 18. July 29. Born Feb. 11, 1827, a daughter of George and Catharine (Sheed) Thomas.

434. **Sarah Catharine Thomas.** 1, l. vi, 1. Aug. 14. Born Sept. 5, 1831. Same parents.

435. **Christian Rudy.** 1, r. xvi, 12. Sept. 4. Born in Warwick, 1763. Son of Henry Rudy. Married Elizabeth Weller.

436. **Beatus Fetter.** 1, r. vi, 6. Sept. 25.

437. **Caroline Sophia Regennas.** 1, l. vi, 2. Oct. 3. Born April 22, 1828, a daughter of John Jacob and Susanna (Kreiter) Regennas.

438. **Matthew Muecke.** 1, r. xx, 13. Oct. 4. Born in Gnadenthal, near Nazareth, March 9, 1755. In 1782 he married Catharina Blickensderfer.

439. **Anna Maria Kapp,** m.n. Korz. 1, l. xvii, 15. Oct. 12. Born in Wohr, Hesse-Darmstadt, Aug. 19, 1742. Wife of John George Kapp.

440. **Mary Ann Regennas.** 1, l. vi, 3. Oct. 14. Born Oct. 14, 1830, a daughter of John Jacob Regennas, farmer.

441. **Hannah Reichel,** m.n. Parsons. 1, l. xx, 16. Nov. 13. She was born in Duffield, England, March 5, 1787. Wife of the Rev. Charles Frederick Reichel, Pastor in Lancaster. One son, Charles Parsons Reichel.

442. **Jacob Theodore Meyer.** 1, r. vi, 7. Dec. 1, Born Nov. 26, 1830, a son of Jonas Meyer, tinsmith.

1833.

443. **Simon Augustus Miller.** 1, r. vi, 8. Jan. 1. A son of Jacob and Barbara (Porter) Miller, aged nearly five years.

444. **Abraham Reinke.** 1, r. xix, 13. Feb. 16. Presbyter. He was born in Philadelphia, June 15, 1752. His parents were the Rev. Abraham and Sarah (Stockberg) Reinke. From 1783 to 1786 he was the Spiritual Superintendent of the Single Brethren in Lititz; was Warden of the Married Members of this congregation in 1790, and passed the last seventeen years of his life as assistant-pastor thereof, during which time he was a welcome preacher in almost every religious denomination in Lancaster Co. He served as the pastor of various congregations,—Heidelberg, Pa., Hope, N. J., Lancaster, twice, and Nazareth, twice. In 1786 he married the widow Maria Sophia Reichelt, m.n. Rudolph, who died in 1816. His second wife was Sarah Joanna (Green) Reich. Of six children from his first marriage he was survived by Samuel and Johanna Augusta.

445. **Lisetta Lichtenthaeler.** 1, l. x, 13. April 2. Born March 26, 1806, a daughter of Adolph Lichtenthaeler. Unmarried.

446. **Beata Levering.** 1, l. vi, 4. April 3.

447. **Caroline Augusta Rudy.** 1, l. vi, 5. April 3. Aged two years. Daughter of Jacob Benjamin and Susanna (Kraemer) Rudy.

448. **Alice Ann Tshudy.** 1, l. vi, 6. April 20. Born Aug. 5, 1829, a daughter of Jacob and Johanna Caroline (Levering) Tshudy.

269

449. **Elizabeth Susanna Levering,** m.n. Carpenter. 1, l. iii, 16. April 24.
Born in Earl Township, 1804. Second wife of John Levering,
merchant.
450. **Mary Margaret Rank.** 1, l. vi, 7. Aged eight months. Daughter of
Michael and Mary Margaret (Shelly) Rank.
451. **Samuel Grosh Thomas.** 1, r. vi, 9. Sept. 21. Aged four months.
452. **Rosina Cassler.** 1, l. xvi, 15. Sept. 27. Born in Bethlehem, Nov. 8,
1750, a daughter of David Tannenberg, organ-builder, and wife of
William Cassler.
453. **Maria Elizabeth Eichler (Frevel).** 1, l. xix, 16. Sept. 29. Born in
1771. Second wife of Gottlieb Eichler. One son, Jonathan.
454. **Christian Fischer.** 1, r. xviii, 13. Nov. 9. Born in Lebanon Co.,
1772. Married Catharine Meyer. Six children.
455. **Angelica Louisa Kreiter.** 1, l. vi, 8. Dec. 24. Six months old.
Daniel Kreiter's daughter.

1834.

456. **Maria Salome Thomas.** 1, l. ix, 13. Jan. 17. Born in Lititz, 1761,
a daughter of John Thomas, baker. Unmarried Sister.
457. **Edward Reuben Fielis.** 1, r. vi, 10. Feb. 11. Born in 1827; son of
Peter Fielis.
458. **John Miller.** 1, r. xvii, 13. March 23. Born in Nazareth, 1760.
Married Anna Maria Frederick. Two sons and two daughters.
459. **Susanna Rosina Grosh.** 1, l. vi, 9. March 26. Daughter of Charles
A. Grosh. Aged five years.
460. **Adolph Lichtenthaeler.** 1, r. xvi, 13. April 5. He was born in
Rodenbach, near Neuwied, Germany, July 18, 1769. Came to Lancaster 1790, and to Lititz in 1792, in both places following his trade
of carpentry. On November 16, 1795, he married Elizabeth Knauss
of Bethlehem. He was survived by eight of fourteen children, of
whom two, Christian and Abraham, became Moravian ministers.
461. **Jacob Fetter.** 1, r. xx, 14. Aug. 20. Born in Lancaster, 1784. Married Mary Margaret Ermert. Of twelve children he was survived
by Jacob George, Margaret, Edward, Ann, and Hermann. A chair-
maker, in Warwick.
462. **Daniel Rickert.** 1, r. xix, 14. Aug. 28. Born in Manor Township,
Jan. 1, 1776. In 1802 he married Magdalena Goepfert. His sons
John, Jacob Henry, William, Hermann, and Ferdinand survived
him. A day-laborer, living in Warwick.
463. **Henrietta Wilhelmina Miller.** 1, l. vi, 10. Sept. 29. Daughter of
Jacob and Anna Wilhelmina (Kreiter) Miller. One year old.
464. **Elizabeth Kreiter.** 1, l. xviii, 16. Oct. 22. Born at Muddy Creek,
April 19, 1771, a daughter of Conrad and Anna Catharina (Heil)
Westhaefer. Wife of Frederick Peter Kreiter.
465. **Emma Albertina Ricksecker.** 1, l. vi, 11. Oct. 25. Infant daughter
of John Ricksecker.
466. **Christian Frederick.** 1, r. xviii, 14. Dec. 13. Born in Warwick,
Aug. 4, 1775. Married Christina Goepfert, who died in 1815. His
second wife was Magdalena Goettman.

467. **Frederick Meyer.** I, r. xvii, 14. Dec. 16. Born in Heidelberg, Pa., 1753. Married Catharine Faber. Lived near Lititz.

468. **Sophia Stauffer.** I, l. viii, 13. Dec. 18. Unmarried Sister. Born 1806, in Lancaster.

1835.

469. **Anna Catharina Schroeter.** I, l. iv, 16. Feb. 23. She was born in Walthershausen, Gotha, May 10, 1765. Wife of the Rev. Carl Frederick Schroeter.

470. **Michael Rank.** I, r. xvi, 14. April 18. Born in Earl Township, Dec. 30, 1802, a son of Samuel Rank. In 1828 he married Mary Margaret Shelly. Of three children he was survived by Matilda and Nathaniel Henry. He was a physician, living in Lexington, about three miles from Lititz. Studied medicine with his father-in-law.

471. **Godfrey Albright.** I, r. xx, 15. May 25. Born in Lititz, 1782. Son of Andrew Albright. Married Elizabeth Romig. His sons were Orlando, Reuben Orth, and William.

472. **Amelia Catharine Hamm.** I, l. vi, 12. Aug. 5. Infant daughter of John Hamm, tobacconist.

473. **Greenbury Pettycourt.** I, r. xi, 12. Sept. 11. Unmarried. He was born Sept. 5, 1748. His father and mother—devout people—kept a public house eight miles hitherward from Georgetown, Md. Becoming acquainted with the Brethren and spiritually influenced by the preaching of Brother Powell, in Carroll's Manor, he came to Lititz, in 1772, and here joined the Brotherhood. Having acquired some knowledge of carpentry, he assisted in the re-building of the congregation mill (destroyed by fire in 1775) and the erection of our church, in 1787; but his service thereafter was that of a general utility man in the community—"making a partition for Brother Benade," candle-boxes for the chandler, a "slay" for Brother Eggert (the Warden) ; ringing the noon-hour bell, winding the town-clock, keeping the fire-engine in repair, etc. Well-authenticated accounts of his uncommon physical agility and strength have come down to us ; we know, too, that he had a charming way with children,—so that Greenbury striding down the street with little boys and girls clustered about or clinging to him was, in that time, a not unfamiliar sight; and we have the word of Bishop Benade for it that he was a beautiful character—simple, true-hearted, ever-helpful, and a devoted Christian. The last few years of his long life he passed in the home and companionship of his old friend Martin Hansen.

474. **Oliver Milton Hackman.** I, r. xv, 17. Sept. 17. Three months old.

475. **Michael Christian Kreiter.** I, r. xix, 15. Sept. 24. Born Nov. 2, 1764, near Lancaster. Married Regina Bieler, 1786. Survived by eight children.

476. **Catharine Klein,** m.n. Fielis. I, l. xvii, 16. Nov. 2. Born in 1815. A daughter of Peter Fielis. Non-Moravian.

477. **John William Kraemer.** I, r. xviii, 15. Dec. 11. Born in Lancaster, April 17, 1803. A son of John Kraemer, cooper, and Catharine, m. n. Scheib. Married Maria Rachel Kreiter.

1836.

478. **Anna Renata Opitz.** 1, l. xii, 14. Jan. 17. Unmarried Sister. Born in Nazareth, 1751.
479. **Henrietta Sophia Fielis.** 1, l. vi, 13. March 9. Born Oct. 2, 1829, a daughter of Peter and Magdalena (Manderbach) Fielis.
480. **Frederick Peter Kreiter.** 1, r. xvii, 15. March 17. He was born in Manor Township, near Lancaster, Sept. 21, 1754, the third son of Peter and Anna Maria (Kohn) Kreiter. In 1788 he married Catharine Leinbach. His sons were Samuel and Daniel; his daughters, Rebecca and Susanna. His second wife, 1810, was Elizabeth Westhaefer.
481. **Peter Ricksecker.** 1, r. xvi, 15. April 30. Born near Lititz, Dec. 30, 1770. Married Margaret Frederick. No children. A shoemaker living in Warwick.
482. **Maria Louisa Kreiter.** 1, l. xvi, 16. May 8. Born in Lititz, July 19, 1798, a daughter of Peter Lennert, and wife of Daniel Kreiter. Of six children, she was survived by Caroline and William Eugene.
483. **Beatus Rickert.** 1, r. xvii, 17. May 20. Son of John Rickert.
484. **Elizabeth Lerch.** 1, l. xi,15. June 8. Unmarried Sister. Born in Northampton Co., 1752.
485. **Maria Louisa Hamm.** 1, l. vi, 14. July 12. Born in Warwick, Feb. 16, 1828, a daughter of John Hamm.
486. **Samuel Frey.** 1, r. x, 12. Oct. 7. Born in 1818. A Non-Moravian.
487. **Eliza Fredericka Hamm.** 1, l. vi, 15. Oct. 16. Daughter of John Hamm. Aged one year, five months.
488. **Mary Agnes Christ.** 1, l. vii, 14. Oct. 30. Daughter of John Rudolph Christ, weaver and dyer. Aged 10 months.

1837.

489. **Maria Salome Geitner.** 1, l. x, 14. March 16. Unmarried Sister. Born in Bethlehem, Dec. 22, 1766.
490. **Martin Hansen.** 1, r. ix, 11. April 5. Unmarried. He was born in the Parish of Dreslette, on the Island of Fuehnen, Denmark, Oct. 22, 1763. Came to this country with his friend Hans Petersen in 1802. A manufacturer of snuff,—especially, "Hansen's Aromatic Cephalick Snuff, which," his business circular states, "is an excellent remedy for the headache and every description of cold in the head. It has likewise been tried with good effect for the toothache." He peddled, with horse and wagon, throughout the state.
491. **Beata Kreiter.** 1, l. vii, 15. April 12.
492. **John Philip Bachman.** 1, r. ii, 1. Nov. 15. Born in Kreuzburg, Thuringia, April 22, 1762. Came to this country to be an assistant of David Tannenberg, organ-builder, in Lititz, and, later, became his partner in the business. In 1793 he married Anna Maria Tannenberg, who died in 1799. In 1800 he married Susanna Elizabeth Albright. By this marriage the children surviving him were Christian, Helen, Amelia, Cornelius and Cyrus.

493. **John Henry Gottlob Heyne.** 1, r. ix, 12. Dec. 20. Born in Ronne-
berg, Voigtland, Sept. 17, 1755. Came to America in 1792. Cook
in the Brethren's House. Unmarried.

1838.

494. **Maria Elizabeth Geitner,** m.n. Kreiter. 1, l. ii, 1. Feb. 18. Born in
Hempfield Township, May 14, 1763. Wife of John George Geitner,
Jr.

495. **John Hamm.** 1, r. ii, 2. March 28. Born in Alsatia. Lived in Warwick. Aged 84 years.

496. **Anna Magdalena Meyer.** 1, l. ix, 14. July 7. Unmarried Sister.
Born near Philadelphia, Oct. 12, 1757. Served many years as the
Pflegerin in the Lititz Sisters' House. A daughter of Dr. Adolph
Meyer.

497. **Catharine Fritsch.** 1, l. viii, 14. July 16. Unmarried Sister. Born
in Gnadenthal, near Nazareth, 1755.

498. **Elizabeth Rudy,** m.n. Weller. 1, l. ii, 2. July 27. Born in Graceham, Md., June 1, 1762. Wife of Christian Rudy.

499. **Christina Kiesel.** 1, l. xii, 15. Nov. 6. Unmarried Sister. Born at
Kissel Hill, near Lititz, Dec. 10, 1760.

500. **Anna Christina Kreiter.** 1, l. xi, 15. Dec. 11. Unmarried Sister.
Born Dec. 13, 1752, a daughter of Peter and Maria (Hirschy)
Kreiter.

1839.

501. **Rachel Ricksecker,** m.n. Frederick. 1, l. ii, 3. Jan. 9. Born in
Donegal, Pa., 1759. Wife of John Ricksecker, who died in 1813.

502. **Orlando Alexander Albright.** 1, r. xii, 13. Unmarried. Born in
Warwick, June 11, 1820. A son of Gottfried Albright.

503. **Peter Grosh.** 1, r. ii, 3. March 26. He was born in Hempfield
Township, Aug. 6, 1774. A son of John Valentine and Barbara
(Sandmann) Grosh. April 20, 1800, he married Maria Catharina
Conrad. They had seven sons and three daughters. Charles
Augustus (1802), Andrew (1805), Timothy (1808), and John
(1816), lived in Lititz; Abraham (1819), in Bethlehem.

504. **Rachel Petersen (Ricksecker).** 1, l. ii, 4. April 8. Born near
Lititz, 1783. Wife of Hans Petersen.

505. **Emma Elizabeth Hackman.** 1, l. vii, 16. Sept. 1. Aged 10 weeks.

1840.

506. **Caroline Lennert.** 1, l. vi, 16. Feb. 3. Aged eight weeks. Daughter
of Ferdinand Lennert.

507. **Susanna Rudy.** 1, l. ii, 5. Feb. 7. Born in Lancaster, 1794. A
daughter of Michael Kraemer, and wife of Jacob Benjamin Rudy.

508. **Israel Immanuel Sturgis.** 1, r. xiii, 18. May 17. Born Oct. 23,
1837. Son of Alexander Sturgis.

509. **Regina Kreiter,** m.n. Bieler. 1, l. ii, 6. May 19. Born in Hebron,
Lebanon Co., Dec. 17, 1767. Wife of Michael Christian Kreiter.

510. **Maria Augusta Eichler,** m.n. Becker. 1, l. ii, 7. July 15. Born Dec.
31, 1798. Wife of Abraham Eichler. Mother of Simon Eichler.

511. **Arthur Augustus Christ.** 1, r. v, 1. Dec. 29. Aged two years. A son of Augustus and Clementina (Kluge) Christ.

1841.

512. **John Frederick Loeffler.** 1, r. ii, 4. Feb. 20. A Deacon of the Church. He was born in Weil, Würtemberg, Sept. 29, 1771. United with the Brethren in Nisky. Came to America in 1802, and served as *Pfleger* first here and then in the Bethlehem Brethren's House. He married Caroline Sophia Reichelt. Labored in the Gospel in Bethel and York. Came to Lititz, a second time, in 1827, and served the congregation in various ways.

1842.

513. **Emma Catharine Grosh.** 1, l. vii, 17. Jan. 2. Aged 6 months. Daughter of Charles Grosh.
514. **Elizabeth Albright.** 1, l. ii, 8. Jan. 12. Born in Heidelberg, Pa., Aug. 21, 1786. Wife of Gottfried Albright.
515. **Martha Elizabeth Weber.** 1, l. vi, 17. April 8. Born in Lancaster, 1841, a daughter of Caspar Weber.
516. **William Henry Muecke.** 1, r. v, 2. June 30. Aged two years. Son of Michael and Amelia (Bachman) Muecke.
517. **Ellen Maria Louisa Imhoff.** 1, l. v, 1. Aug. 17. Aged five years. Her mother's maiden name was Graeff.
518. **Maria Belinda Bachman.** 1, l. v, 2. Aug. 27. Aged 4 months. A daughter of the Rev. Christian Henry Bachman.
519. **Elizabeth Kiesel.** 1, l. ii, 9. Sept. 3. She was born near Lititz, July 3, 1782. Daughter of Adam and Christina Kiener, and wife of Abraham Frederick Kiesel.
520. **Sarah Susanna Seaber.** 1, l. v, 3. Oct. 4. Aged twelve years. Daughter of John Jacob Seaber.

1843.

521. **Louisa Dorothea Bachman.** 1, l. ii, 10. Jan. 3. She was born on the Island of St. Croix, where her parents were missionaries, Feb. 10, 1813. Her maiden name was Kitchelt. In 1830 she married the Rev. Henry Christian Bachman, and went with him to New Fairfield, Canada. The Rt. Rev. Henry T. Bachman was one of her sons.
522. **Elizabeth Conn,** m.n. Ackermann. 1, l. ii, 11. Feb. 17. Born 1761, in Lancaster. Wife of Peter Conn.
523. **Renatus Ernst Paulick.** 1, r. xi, 13. April 5. Unmarried. Aged thirty years. Son of John George Paulick.
524. **Sarah Clementina Levering.** 1, l. v, 4. April 6. Daughter of Ferdinand Levering. Aged six years.
525. **Maria Emilie Senft.** 1 l. v, 5. April 22. Daughter of the Rev. Senft, Warden of the congregation. Two years old.
526. **Rufus Justinus Miksch.** 1, r. v, 3. April 29. Aged three months.

527. **Cordelia Hackman.** 1, l. ii, 12. April 30. Born in 1814, a daughter of Peter Abraham Kreiter. Wife of Abraham Hackman of Womelsdorf, Pa.

528. **Theodore Meyers Kreiter.** 1, r. v, 4. May 22. Son of Daniel and Anna Maria (Meyers) Kreiter. Two years old.

529. **Anna Charlotte Frank.** 1, l. xii, 16. Sept. 17. Unmarried Sister. Born in Lancaster, 1785.

530. **Beatus Graeff.** 1, r. vii, 12. Nov. 29. Jacob Graeff's child.

1844.

531. **Cecilia Louisa Miksch.** 1, l. ii, 13. March 17. She was born in Nazareth, June 21, 1817, a daughter of Jacob and Salome Brunner. Wife of James Henry Miksch.

532. **Rebecca Catharine Petersen.** 1, l. x, 15. March 29. Unmarried Sister,—aged twenty years, ten months. Daughter of Hans Petersen.

533. **Caroline Augusta Hull.** 1, l. v, 6. May 23. Daughter of Dr. Hull, —aged two years.

534. **Mary Louisa Thomas.** 1, l. ix, 15. May 29. She was born June 10, 1829. A daughter of George and Catharine (Sheed) Thomas.

535. **Charles Frederick Lennert.** 1, r. v, 5. June 20. Aged one year—a son of Ferdinand Lennert.

536. **Louisa Theresa Grosh.** 1, l. v, 7. Aug. 9. Aged five months. Daughter of Charles Aug. Grosh.

537. **Henry Blickensderfer.** 1, r. v, 6. Aug. 25. Son of Henry Blickensderfer; aged eleven months.

538. **Sarah Frances Lichtenthaeler.** 1, l. v, 8. Aug. 27. Daughter of Samuel Lichtenthaeler; aged three years.

539. **John Erdman Oehme.** 1, r. ii, 5. Sept. 30. Born in Sorau, Saxony, May 22, 1758. Came to America, 1786, and to Lititz in 1800. Married Elizabeth Frevel.

540. **Ellen Elizabeth Rauch.** 1, l. v, 9. Dec. 14. Infant daughter of Edward Rauch.

541. **Samuel Justinus Sturgis.** 1, r. ii, 6. Dec. 21. Born July 23, 1781, in Lebanon. Son of Joseph Sturgis. By trade a potter. For many years the grave-digger here. Aug. 19, 1804, in York, he married Susanna Correll. Seven sons and seven daughters were born to them.

542. **Louisa Elvina Sturgis.** 1, l. v, 10. Dec. 24. Infant daughter of Alexander Sturgis.

543. **Levin Florentin Masslich.** 1, r. x, 13. Dec. 26. A son of Timothy Masslich, aged fourteen years.

1845.

544. **Alice Emilia Bricker.** 1, l. v, 11. Jan. 8. Born in Warwick, a daughter of David Bricker, March 29, 1840.

545. **Peter Anthony Bricker.** 1, r. v, 7. Jan. 8. Aged one year. Son of David and Lucinda (Petersen) Bricker.

546. **Maria Frederica Traeger.** 1, l. v, 12. March 28. Aged four years. Daughter of Aaron and Sarah (Zahm) Traeger.

547. **Immanuel Uriah Oehme.** 1, r. v, 8. May 25. Aged three years. A son of Christian Oehme.
548. **Laura Ann Traeger.** 1, l. v, 13. July 26. Infant daughter of Aaron Traeger.
549. **Michael Kreiter.** 1, r. ii, 7. Oct. 20. Born Dec. 29, 1795. Son of Michael Gottfried Kreiter. Married Anna Matilda Levering.
550. **Susanna Magdalena Rock.** 1, l. ii, 14. Nov. 19. Born Jan. 19, 1783,—a daughter of Daniel Christ. Wife of Jacob Rock.

1846.

551. **Edwin Theodore Grosh.** 1, r. v, 9. Jan. 8. Infant son of Andrew Grosh.
552. **Beatus Lichtenthaeler.** 1, r. v, 10. Feb. 2. Son of Samuel Lichtenthaeler.
553. **Abraham Eichler.** 1, r. ii, 8. Feb. 28. Born June 1, 1796. A son of Gottlieb Eichler. In 1819 he married Maria Augusta Becker, who died in 1840. In 1841 he married Elizabeth Sauter. The cause of his death was apoplexy.
554. **Mary Catharine Bricker.** 1, l. v, 14. June 25. Infant daughter of David Bricker.
555. **Samuel Reinke Beck.** 1, r. ix, 13. July 11. He was born April 12, 1825. A son of John and Augusta (Reinke) Beck. Was a clerk in John Meyers' store, Lancaster. A fine violinist, and organist of the First German Reformed Church in the same city. For the beauty of his voluntaries we have the word of Pastor Glessner.
556. **John Martin Beck** (second). 1, r. ix, 14. Dec. 9, 1834. He was born Oct. 17, 1820. First-born child of the foregoing parents. A pupil in the school of Brother Ernst Bleck, in York, he died there, of typhus fever, and was buried in the graveyard of that congregation; but on July 28, 1846, his remains were exhumed and brought hither to rest beside those of his brother, re-interment taking place the next day.
557. **John Gottlob Kummer.** 1, r. ii, 9. Aug. 6. He was born in Nisky, on the Island of St. Thomas, May 29, 1790. He was the Principal of Linden Hall Seminary, 1826-30, and served in the same capacity from March, 1836, more than seven years in Bethlehem. In 1820 he married Sarah Hinchcliffe. His last service was as Warden of the Lititz Congregation. A son of his, Charles Edward, of Medford, Mass., was formerly Principal of the Bethlehem Parochial School.
558. **Johanna Susanna Lennert,** m.n. Knauss. 1, l. ii, 15. Sept. 5. Born in Bethlehem, Nov. 1, 1773. Wife of John Peter Lennert.
559. **Ellen Frances Rauch.** 1, l. v, 15. Dec. 14. Daughter of Rudolph Rauch. Infant.
560. **Edmund Francis Rickert.** 1, r. i, 1. Infant son of Ferdinand Rickert.

1847.

561. **Anna Maria Ricksecker.** 1, l. viii, 15. Dec.. 31, (1846). Unmarried Sister. Born in 1786.

562. **Abraham Eichler.** 1, r. i. 2 . Jan. 28. Infant son of Simon and Mary Ann (Petersen) Eichler.

563. **Henry Gabriel Traeger.** 1, r. i, 3. Jan. 29. Infant son of Aaron Traeger.

564. **William Kittera Hull.** 1, r. i, 4. April 1. Infant son of Dr. Levi Hull.

565. **Beatus Wolle.** 1, r. i, 5. Apr. 5. Son of Nathaniel and Angelica (Miksch) Wolle.

566. **Charles Augustus Enk.** 1, r. i, 6. Aug. 9. Infant son of Augustus and Matilda (Seaber) Enk.

567. **Henry Clay Christ.** 1, r. i, 7. Aug. 27. Infant son of Augustus Christ.

568. **Mary Frances Grosh.** 1, l. v, 16. Sept. 18. Infant daughter of Andrew Grosh.

569. **Charles Frederick Diehm.** 1, r. i, 8. Sept. 20. Infant son of William Diehm.

570. **Sarah Frances Lichtenthaeler.** 1, l. v, 17. Nov. 6. Infant daughter of Samuel Lichtenthaeler.

571. **Emma Josephine Lennert.** 1, l. i, 1. Nov. 12. Infant daughter of Ferdinand Lennert.

1848.

572. **Aaron Traeger.** 1, r. ii, 10. Jan. 31. Born Aug. 6, 1815. Son of John Gottfried Traeger. In 1840 he married Sarah Zahm, of Lancaster. A chair-maker.

573. **Abraham Frederick Miller.** 1, r. xii, 14. Feb. 3. Unmarried. Aged twenty-eight years.

574. **Clementina Louisa Christ,** m.n. Kluge. 1, l. ii, 16. Feb. 24. She was born in Bethabara, N. C., Aug. 12, 1813. Wife of Augustus Christ.

575. **Anna Regina Grosh,** m.n. Shoenlein. 1, l. iv, 17. March 5. Born July 20, 1775. Wife of Samuel Grosh. No children.

576. **John Kraemer.** 1, r. xii, 15. March 14. Unmarried. Born in Lancaster, March 31, 1811. Son of John and Catharine Kraemer.

577. **Elizabeth Traeger,** m.n. Hall. 1, l. iv, 18. April 2. Born in Bethlehem, Feb. 14, 1780. Wife of John Gottfried Traeger. She was for many years the faithful and loved school-mistress, here, of the little boys.

578. **Henrietta Protzman.** 1, l. xi, 16. April 12. Unmarried Sister. Born in Graceham, Md., Oct. 25, 1802. Daughter of Lewis and Elizabeth (Rouser) Protzman.

579. **Sophia Augusta Grosh,** m.n. Rauch. 1, l. iii, 17. May 22. Born in Warwick, Feb. 28, 1823. Wife of Andrew Grosh.

580. **Christian Hall.** 1, r. ii, 11. June 30. He was born in Bethlehem, May 10, 1775, a son of James Hall. Married Catharine Protzman. Five children. He was at one time the landlord of the Lititz Inn, engaging also in the repairing of clocks and watches; later he kept a small grocery store.

581. **John Hamm** (second). 1, r. ii, 12. July 24. Born in Elsheim, near Mainz, Dec. 21, 1798. Married Louisa Dinges. He had seven children, but was survived only by Lisetta Margaretha, wife of Jacob Weitzel. A tobacconist.

582. **Sophia Augusta Grosh.** 1, l. i, 2. July 27. Infant daughter of Sophia (Rauch) Grosh.

583. **Abraham Frederick Kissel.** 1, r. iv, 13. Aug. 7. Born Jan. 6, 1772, at Kissel Hill. Married Elizabeth Kiener. Seven children.

584. **Abner William Diehm.** 1, r. i, 10. Aug. 25. Aged three years. Son of William Diehm.

585. **Ella Clavilla Paulick.** 1, l. i, 3. Sept. 16. Infant daughter of Andrew and Barbara (Graeff) Paulick.

586. **Harriet Conrad.** 1, l. x, 16. Sept. 23. Aged twelve years, six months.

587. **William Kittera Hull.** 1, r. i, 9. Aug. 13. Aged one year. Son of Dr. Hull.

588. **Beata Lichtenthaeler.** 1, l. i, 4. Oct. 17. Infant daughter of Samuel Lichtenthaeler.

589. **Charles Edwin Ricksecker.** 1, r. iii, 13. Oct. 14. Born Feb. 27, 1820, in Lititz. Married Caroline Sturgis. One son.

590. **Ellen Louisa Grosh.** 1, l. i, 5. Nov. 18. Aged one year. Daughter of Charles Augustus Grosh.

591. **Andrew Ferdinand Paulick.** 1, r. iv, 14. Nov. 20. Born 1826. Married Barbara Graeff.

592. **Mary Frances Hull.** 1, l. ix, 16. Nov. 23. Aged eleven years and three months. A daughter of Dr. Levi Hull.

593. **Maria Magdalena Rauch.** 1, l. iii, 18. Nov. 25. She was born in Heidelberg, Pa., April 20, 1789. Her parents were Jacob and Rosina Romig. In 1812 she was married to Christian Henry Rauch. Four sons and four daughters.

1849.

594. **Laura Aurelia Kreiter.** 1, l. i, 6. Jan. 1. Aged eight years. Daughter of Charles H. Kreiter.

595. **William Eberman Lennert.** 1, r. i, 11. April 11. Aged eight years. Son of Ferdinand Lennert.

596. **Sarah Ann Keller,** m.n. Young. 1, l. ii, 17. April 14. Born in Lancaster, Aug. 25, 1819. Wife of Edward Keller.

597. **Caroline Sophia Loeffler,** m.n. Reichelt. 1, l. ii, 18. June 20. Born at Herrnhut, Island of St. Thomas, Oct. 13, 1784. Wife of the Rev. John Frederick Loeffler.

598. **Ferdinand Theophilus Keller.** 1, r. i, 12. July 23. Infant son of Edward Keller.

599. **Charles Kittera Hull.** Aug. 18. Nine weeks old. Probably buried in the grave of his brother, (No. 587).

600. **John Grosh.** 1, r. xi, 14. Sept. 14. Unmarried. Born in Hempfield Township, a son of Peter Grosh, May 5, 1816. His mother's maiden name was Conrad.

601. **Anna Hannah McIlhenny.** 1, l. i, 7. Sept. 19. Aged one year.

602. **John Rickert.** 1, r. iii, 14. Dec. 3. Born near Lititz, June 6, 1806, a son of Daniel Rickert. He was the teacher of advanced pupils in John Beck's Academy; a man of varied talents and high accomplishments. The older towns-people remember with pleasure the beauty and ingenuity displayed on his Christmas "putzes." Father of the Rev. Alfred Addison Rickert.

604. **Maria Sophia Ricksecker.** 1, l. viii, 16. Dec. 17. Unmarried Sister. Born Oct. 20, 1825. Daughter of John and Fredericka (Fisher) Ricksecker.

1850.

605. **John Jacob Regennas.** 1, r. ii, 13. Jan. 9. Born in Lampenberg, Canton Basle, Switzerland, July 7, 1780. Came with his parents to America in 1803. Married Susanna Kreiter, 1815. Of his nine children three sons and three daughters survived him. Father of the Rev. John Jacob Regennas.

606. **Cornelia Eleanora Miksch.** 1, l. i, 8. Jan. 9. Daughter of James Henry and Matilda (Kreiter) Miksch. Born May 23, 1846.

607. **Charles Henry Levering.** 1, r. i, 14. Jan. 15. Son of Lewis Ferdinand Levering. Aged two years.

608. **Anna Fetter,** m.n. Roesler. 1, l. xx, 17. Jan. 23. Born March 11, 1815. Wife of Samuel Fetter.

609. **Caroline Elizabeth Kreiter.** 1, l. i, 9. Feb. 12. Infant daughter of Carl Rudolph Kreiter.

610. **Laura Elizabeth Flory.** 1, l. i, 10. April 13. Aged five years. Daughter of John Flory.

611. **Sarah Caroline Diehm.** 1, l. i, 11. May 1. Infant daughter of William Diehm.

612. **Beatus Sturgis.** 1, r. i, 15. June 18. Son of Alexander Sturgis.

613. **Verona Sturgis,** m.n. Huber. 1, l. xix, 17. June 18. Born in Upper Culm, Canton Aargau, Switzerland, May 2, 1812. Wife of James Alexander Sturgis.

614. **Samuel Grosh.** 1, r. ii, 14. July 12. Born May 14, 1768, a son of Philip and Anna Margaretha (Rank) Grosh. For many years he kept the village store; was a prominent, progressive citizen, and filled various offices in the Church. He was at one time a member of the State Legislature. A man of distinguished presence.

615. **Sarah Frances Rauch.** 1, l. i, 12. July 15. Infant daughter of Edward H. Rauch.

616. **Adelaide Bechler.** 1, l. i, 14. July 24. Infant daughter of the Rev. Julius Bechler.

617. **John Kaufman Hull.** 1, r. viii, 12. Aug. 4. Aged one year. Son of Dr. Levi Hull.

618. **Alfred Taylor Grosh.** 1, r. viii, 13. Aug. 15. Infant son of Charles Augustus Grosh.

619. **Magdalena Miksch,** m.n. Proskiofski. 1, l. xviii, 17. Sept. 11. Born in Northampton Co., Pa., July 6, 1794. Served with her husband, Christian Miksch, on the Indian Mission, from 1830 until his death in 1845.

620. **Margaret Ricksecker,** m.n. Frederick. 1, l. xvii, 17. Oct. 10. Born Oct. 22, 1769. Wife of Peter Ricksecker. No children.

1851.

621. **Martin Jacob Gingrich.** 1, r. x, 14. March 7. Unmarried. Born Aug. 13. 1831. Son of Jacob Gingrich.
622. **Josephine Reinhart.** 1, l. i, 15. March 20. Infant daughter of Israel Reinhart, landlord of the Lititz Inn.
623. **Anna Mary Kreiter,** m.n. Meyer. 1, l. xvii, 17. April 20. Born in York, Oct. 23, 1800. Wife of Daniel Kreiter.
624. **Lisetta Virginia Graeff.** 1, l. i, 13. June 19. Daughter of Jacob Graeff. Aged three months.
625. **Albert Blickensderfer.** 1, r. vii, 14. July 30. Infant son of Henry Blickensderfer.
626. **Morris Jefferson Flory.** 1, r. viii, 15. Aug. 5. Aged four years. Son of John Flory.
627. **Camilla Eulalia Regennas.** 1, l. i, 16. Aug. 13. Aged three years. Daughter of William Henry Regennas.
628. **Laura Emily Christ.** 1, l. i, 17. Sept. 1. Aged three years. Daughter of Francis W. Christ.
629. **Anna Maria Paulick,** m.n. Rudy. 2, l. xxiii, 16. Sept. 11. Born in Warwick, 1783. Daughter of Henry Rudy. Wife of John George Paulick.
630. **Anna Mary Rank.** 1, l. xii, 17. Oct. 12. Unmarried Sister. Born Dec. 5, 1768, near New Holland, Lancaster Co.

1852.

631. **Catharine Mary Kreiter.** 1, l. i, 18. Feb. 6. Infant daughter of Solomon Kreiter.
632. **Agnes Sophia Frederick.** 1, l. xv, 18. Feb. 29. Infant daughter of George Lewis Frederick.
633. **Mary Louisa Lennert.** 1, l. xiv, 18. March 25. Seven years old. Daughter of Ferdinand Lennert.
634. **Emma Ida Reinhart.** 1, l. xiii, 19. April 1. Three years old.
635. **Charles Frederick Christ.** 1, r. v, 11. April 15. Son of Augustus Christ.
636. **John Kraemer.** 1, r. iv, 15. July 8. Born in Lancaster, July 15, 1772. Married Anna Catharine Sheib. Three sons and seven daughters. A cooper.
637. **Charles Albert Grosh.** 1, r. vi, 12. Infant son of Charles Augustus Grosh.
638. **Beata Metzger.** 2, l. x, 16. June 16.
639. **Sarah Elizabeth Feather.** 2, l. x, 15. Aug. 1.
640. **Maria Sophia Dieter.** 1, l. xi, 17. Aug. 26. Unmarried Sister. Aged fifty-seven years.
641. **Frederick Keller.** 1, r. iii, 15. Oct. 3. He was born in Fredericktown, Maryland, July 15, 1794. Married Anna Maria Kraemer. A saddler.

5

280

642. **Catharine Kreiter,** m.n. Boehmer. 2, l. xxiii, 15. Oct. 3. Born
March 14, 1792. Wife of Christian Kreiter.
643. **Matthias Tshudy.** 1, r. ii, 15. Oct. 25. He was born in Lititz, Aug.
9, 1771, a son of Christian and Eva Barbara (Kiesel) Tshudy. Left
an orphan at an early age, he was adopted by Peter Kreiter and
treated as a son. In his eighth year he was placed in the Brethren's
house under the special guardianship of Brother Chitty, superintendent of the weaving department. June 10, 1792, he married
Catharine Blickensderfer. Besides his trade of weaving, he caried
on, very extensively, the manufacture of chip hats and bonnets,—
made nowhere else in America. In 1848 he and his wife celebrated
their Golden Wedding. He took an active interest in the affairs of
the congregation, was a frequent member of the *Aufseher Collegium,*
a choir-singer and trombonist, and in 1837 presented a new pulpit
to the church. At his own expense he laid out, planted and enclosed
the church-square. Of his six children he was survived by one son
and two daughters.

1853.

644. **Hortensia Louisa Christ.** 1, l. x, 17. March 6. Aged twelve years.
Daughter of Augustus and Clementina (Kluge) Christ.
645. **Edward Hubley Levering.** 1, r. vii, 13. Aged three years. Son of
Ferdinand Levering.
646. **Maria Theresa Wolle.** 2, l. xxii, 16. April 8 . She was born June 3,
1799, in Salem, N. C., a daughter of Gottlieb and Mary Magdalena
(Transu) Shober. Wife of the Rev. Peter Wolle, who was for
many years pastor of the Lititz Congregation. Six children.
647. **Eugenia Rickert.** 2, l. x, 14. Aug. 3. Daughter of John Rickert.
Aged ten years.
648. **Magdalena Fielis.** 2, l. xx, 15. Aug. 3. Born Oct. 5, 1796. Wife of
Peter Fielis. Her maiden name was Manderbach.
649. **Mary Ellet.** 1, l. ix, 17. Aug. 30. Unmarried. Born in Tyrone
County, Ireland, 1830. A domestic of Linden Hall.
650. **Emma Cornelia Bechler.** 2, l. xiii, 14. Sept. 17. Born in Nazareth,
May 20, 1816. Her parents were Dr. Henry Benjamin and Anna
Maria (Otto) Schmidt. Wife of the Rev. Julius Bechler, Warden
of the Lititz congregation. Of her five children, two survived her.
651. **Adelaide Constantia Bachman.** 1, l. viii, 17. Sept. 26. Unmarried
Sister. Born in Millerstown, Lebanon Co., Oct. 19, 1831. A daughter
of the Rev. Christian Henry Bachman. Teacher in Linden Hall,
and solo soprano of the church-choir.

1854.

652. **Mary Caroline Buch.** 2, l. x, 13. July 25. Aged eight months.
Daughter of Elias and Maria (Grosh) Buch.
653. **Magdalena Schmidt,** m.n. Knauss. 2, l. xiii, 13. Sept. 11. Born in
Bethlehem, Dec. 2, 1782. Wife of Anton Schmidt, who died in 1823.

1855.

654. **Catharine Hall,** m.n. Protzman. 2, l. xxii, 14. March 21. Born near Graceham, Md., July 31, 1776. Wife of Christian Hall.

655. **Catharine Louisa Kreiter.** 2, l. xvi, 16. April 9. Unmarried Sister. Born near Lancaster, Oct. 18, 1773. At the consecration of the Lititz Moravian Church, Aug. 13, 1787, when she was thirteen years old, she was baptized, in a special meeting, by Bishop Ettwein, "in the presence of more than two thousand people."

656. **Elinor Cecilia Rickert.** 2, l. xvi, 15. Oct. 8. She was born Nov. 19, 1837, a daughter of John and Juliet (Rock) Rickert. A beautiful girl. With the opening words of his funeral discourse, Bishop Samuel Reinke—true to his originality—held to view a half-blown rose—making earnest application from the sweet similitude of departed loveliness and broken flower.

657. **Maria Wilhelmina Werner.** 2, l. xvi, 14. Nov. 18. Unmarried Sister. Aged seventy-two years.

658. **Mary Reichel,** m.n. Parsons. 2, l. xxiii, 12. July 9. Wife of the Rev. Gotthold Benjamin Reichel. She was born in Mansfield, England, Dec. 14, 1792. Died in York, Pa., and was buried there. Re-interred Nov. 29.

659. **Alice Augusta Rauch.** 2, l. xv, 16. Dec. 14. Aged twelve years and ten months. Daughter of Rudolph Rauch.

660. **Augustus Kreiter Kraemer.** 3, l. xvi, 1. Dec. 18. Unmarried. Aged twenty-five years. Son of William and Rachel (Kreiter) Kraemer.

1856.

661. **Samuel Andrew Huebener.** 3, l. xvi, 2. Jan. 27. Born in Graceham, Md., March 3, 1837, a son of the Rev. Samuel and Salome (Tshudy) Huebener. He was a student of fine promise in the Moravian Theological Seminary, then located in Philadelphia, and had come home for the Christmas holidays, dying here of typhoid fever.

662. **Edward Samuel Enck.** 1, r. vi, 14. Feb. 29. Infant.

663. **Beata Christ.** 2, l. ix, 16. March 14. Daughter of Francis Christ.

664a. **Gertrude Eugenia Rickert.** 2, l. ix, 15. March 23. Infant daughter of Ferdinand Rickert.

664b. **Sarah Elizabeth Cox.** 2, l. ix, 14. April 6.

665. **John Shoenlein.** 3, l. xiii, 1. April 27. Born in Lititz, May 31, 1783. Son of Leonhard Shoenlein. Married Elizabeth Ricksecker.

666. **Sarah Caroline Huebener.** 2, l. xxii, 13. Sept. 22. She was born Sept. 29, 1832, a daughter of Jacob and Caroline (Harbaugh) Tshudy. First wife of Dr. Obadiah T. Huebener.

667. **Jacob Miller.** 3, l. xxiii, 2. Dec. 17. Lived near Lititz. Non-Moravian. Aged sixty-six years.

1857.

668. **Edgar Eugene Christ.** i, r. vi, 11. Jan. 28. Son of Augustus Christ. Aged three years. Scarlet fever.
669. **Beatus Bear.** Son of William L. Bear. i, r. v, 12. March 13.
670. **Martha Elizabeth Eichler.** 2, l. ix, 13. March 26. Daughter of Simon Eichler. Aged one year. Scarlet fever.
671. **Ada Lavinia Conrad.** 2, l. ix, 12. April 6. Two years. Scarlet fever.
672. **Mary Theodora Bear.** 2, l. ix, 11. April 9. Daughter of William L. and Mary (Young) Bear. Four years old. Died of a malignant fever.
673. **Samuel Webster Sturgis.** i, r. v, 13. April 17. Infant son of Edward and Rosanna Sturgis. One year, ten months old. Scarlet fever.
674. **Joseph Allison McIlhenny.** i, r. v, 14. May 1. Two years. Croup.
675. **Anna Rosina Rauch.** 2, l. xxii, 12. May 11. She was born in Gnadenthal, near Nazareth, Feb. 25, 1787, a daughter of the Rev. Andreas Busse. May 22, 1826, she married the widower John William Rauch, of Lititz.
676. **William Albert Sturgis.** i, r. i, 13. Jan. 13. Son of Edward Sturgis. Died of scarlet fever, aged four years.
677. **Samuel Harvey Buch.** 3, l. x, 1. June 13. Infant son of Elias and Maria Buch.
678. **Sarah Catharine Buch.** 2, l. x, 12. Aug. 27. Daughter of Israel Buch. Infant.
679. **Clara Stark.** 2, l. x, 11. Sept. 4. Infant daughter of Catharine Stark. Non-Moravian.
680. **John Gottlieb Fischer.** 3, l. xxiii, 3. Oct. 12. Born at Frühholzheim, Germany, 1825. Came to America, 1850. Married Maria Herman.
681. **Infant son of John Oehme.** 3, l. x, 2. Oct. 25.
682. **Louisa Fredericka Ricksecker.** 2, l. xxiii, 11. Dec. 30. Her maiden name was Fisher. She was born Aug. 24, 1793, at Hope, Surinam, where her parents were missionaries. Wife of John Ricksecker.

1858.

683. **Walter Edward Christ.** 3, l. x, 3. Jan. 4. Son of Francis William Christ. Aged five years.
684. **Jacob Greider.** 3, l. xxiii, 4. Feb. 3. He was born March 19, 1788, a son of Michael and Magdalena (Grosh) Kreiter. Married Juliana Christ. Four sons and three daughters. By trade a shoemaker. Played the bassoon in the church-music.
685. **Hedwig Aurelia Christ,** m.n. Rauch. 2, l. xxii, 11. Feb. 5. Born Dec. 10, 1817. Teacher in Linden Hall Seminary from 1837 to 1849. Wife of Augustus Christ. Daughter of Heinrich Gottfried Rauch.
686. **Anna Magdalena Fetter,** m.n. Goodyear. 2, l. xxiii, 10. March 13. Born June 3, 1766. Married, in Lancaster, the widower Jacob Fetter.
687. **Ellen Louisa Rauch.** 2, l. x, 10. April 15. Infant daughter of Francis Rauch.

688. **Emma Elizabeth Bicking.** 2, l. ix, 10. April 15. Daughter of James M. Bicking. Aged six years.

689. **Elizabeth Lichtenthaeler,** m.n. Knauss. 2, l. xxii, 10. June 21. Born in Bethlehem, Nov. 26. 1775. Wife of Adolph Lichtenthaeler. Died from a cancerous ulcer on her right cheek.

690. **John George Paulick.** 3, l. xxiii, 5. July 14. Born at Jahmen, Upper Lusatia, March 18, 1777. Came to this country, 1805. His first wife, Maria Bauerman, died in 1806. In 1807 he married Maria Verona Rudy. They had three sons and three daughters. He died at the home of his son in Lancaster.

691. **Sarah Louisa Frederick.** 2, l. x, 9. July 20. Aged six years.

692. **Thomas Jefferson Keller.** 3, l. x, 4. Aug. 14. Son of Samuel E. Keller. Aged two years.

693. **Harry Albert Buch.** 3, l. x, 5. Aug. 16. Infant son of Elias and Maria (Grosh) Buch.

694. **Anna Rosina Eck.** 2, l. ix, 9. Aug. 26. Infant daughter of Martin and Gertrude Eck.

695. **Samuel Keller.** 3, l. xxiii, 6. Sept. 7. Born in Lancaster, 1794. Married Elizabeth Erb. Four sons and seven daughters. Miller at the old Lititz Mill. Died suddenly of apoplexy.

696. **Lewis Eichelberger.** 3, l. x, 6. Sept. 12. Two months old.

1859.

699. **Beatus Eck.** 3, l. x, 7. Jan. 11.

700. **Beata Feather.** 3, l. x, 8. Jan. 24.

701. **Anna Juliana Christ.** 2, l. xxii, 9. Jan. 27. Born in Lititz, April 20, 1783. Daughter of Peter Christ, and widow of Christian Christ. After the death of her husband in 1828, she moved to Nazareth where she served as sick-nurse in the Hall till 1841 when she returned to Lititz.

702. **John Wellington Buch.** 3, l. x, 8. March 30. Infant son of Joseph and Louisa Buch.

703. **John R. M. Bicking.** 3, l. xxiii, 7. April 17. Born Dec. 11, 1794, in Montgomery Co. He resided five years in Lititz. Died of consumption.

704. **Laura Emily Kryder.** 2, l. ix, 8. March. Daughter of Charles and Olivia Kryder. Remains brought hither from Philadelphia.

705. **Peter Augustus Christ.** 3, l. xxiii, 8. May 3. Born in Lititz, Feb. 13, 1813, a son of Christian Christ. His first wife was Clementina Louisa Kluge. After her death in 1848, he married Hedwig Aurelia Rauch. For twenty-nine years he served as a teacher in John Beck's Lititz Academy. His last illness was a lingering consumption.

706. **Amelia Charity Kummer,** m.n. Reichel. 2, l. xxiii, 8. May 31. Born in Salem, N. C., Dec. 3, 1826. Married to the Rev. Joseph H. Kummer in 1847, and served with him in the missions of St. Cruz and Jamaica seven years; returned to this country in 1854, served the church at Brooklyn, L. I., four years and moved to Lancaster in

1858, where she died "a happy and triumphant death," of brain fever, aged thirty-two years and five months.

707. **Charlotte Sophia Reinke.** 2, l. xxiii, 7. June 20. She was born in Nisky, Germany, Nov. 20, 1802, a daughter of Bishop Christian Gottlieb Hueffel. Came to this country with her parents and only sister in 1818. Married the widower, the Rev. Samuel Reinke, in 1827. With him she served the congregations of Graceham, Lancaster, Nazareth, Bethlehem, twice, York, and Lititz. Their union was blest with seven children, of whom two daughters and one son, the Rt. Rev. Clement Leander Reinke, survived her. "She calmly and sweetly fell asleep in Jesus, in the full hope of a blessed immortality."

708. **Beata Merkle.** 2, l. x, 7. April.

709. **Beatus Smith.** 3, l. x, 9. Sept. 28. Infant son of William and Catharine Smith.

710. **John Harvey Evans.** 3, l. x, 10. Oct. 4. Infant son of John and Susan (Grosh) Evans.

1860.

711. **Josephine Diehm.** 2, l. ix, 7. Jan. 2. Daughter of William Diehm. Died of scarlet fever, aged seven years.

712. **Catherine Blickensderfer,** m.n. Romig. 2, l. xxii, 8. Jan. 3. Born near Emmaus, Jan. 27, 1776. In 1800 she married the widower Matthew Blickensderfer. For many years she served the community far and near as an efficient and energetic midwife. Died of a pectoral fever.

713. **Lewis Parmenio Ricksecker.** 3, l. xxiii, 9. Jan. 3. Born in Lititz, 1813. Son of John Ricksecker. At one time a member of the congregation. Lived last in Columbia, where he was found a corpse in his bed, having been suffocated by a hemorrhage of the lungs.

714. **Joseph Benjamin Shoenlein.** 3, l. xvi, 4. Feb. 12. Born in Lititz, 1810. Son of John Shoenlein. Former member of the church.

715. **Ida Cecilia Diehm.** 2, l. ix, 6. Feb. 22. Daughter of William Diehm. Aged six years.

716. **Samuel Irenaeus Reinke.** 3, l. x, 11. Feb. 25. Born at New Carmel, Jamaica, July 4, 1857, a son of the Rev. Edwin E. Reinke. Died of pneumonia, aged two years.

717. **Eversley Thomas.** 3, l. x, 12. Aug. 12. Infant son of Reynold and Martha Thomas, of Philadelphia. Died while on a visit here with his parents. Aged one year, eight months.

718. **Elizabeth Hambright,** m.n. Brunner. 2, l. xxii, 7. Aug. 27. Born in 1823. Wife of Adam Hambright. One son. Died of consumption.

719. **Harvey S. Kauffman.** 3, l. x, 13. Sept. 22. Infant son of Emmanuel Kauffman.

1861.

720. **Martha Ann Hammer.** 2, l. xxiii, 6. Jan. 31. She was born in Lititz, April 19, 1827, a daughter of John and Johanna Augusta

(Reinke) Beck. Wife of William A. Hammer, of Cressona, Schuylkill Co., where she died of puerperal fever. Her infant, Annie Beck, followed its mother Aug. 12, and was buried in the same grave. She had five children. Before her marriage, a soprano singer in the church-choir.

721. **Margaret Oehme,** m.n. Gernand. 2, l. xxii, 6. Feb. 1. Lived in Lexington, near Lititz. She was in her fifty-ninth year when she died.

722. **Clara Julia Theodora Bechler.** 2, l. x, 6. March 6. Infant daughter of the Rev. Julius and Theodora Bechler.

723. **David Henry Rickert.** 3, l. x, 14. March 9. Infant son of Charles Rickert, of Warwick.

724. **Sarah Ellen Frederick.** 2, l. ix, 5. March 18. Infant.

725. **Maria Catharine Fisher.** 2, l. xxiii, 5. March 30. Born in Heidelberg, Pa., 1784. A widow.

726. **John Junghans.** 3, l. xvi, 5. June 2. Unmarried. Born March 8, 1824, at Friedensfeld, St. Croix.

727. **Caroline Wilhelmina Heiserman.** 2, l. x, 4. July 12. Infant daughter of George and Catharine (Kling) Heiserman.

728. **Israel Hermes Grosh.** 3, l. xvi, 6. Aug. 19. Son of Timothy Grosh. He served his country in the "three months' service" during the Civil War, and contracted a fever in camp from which he died, aged eighteen years.

729. **Elizabeth Miller,** m.n. Grosh. 2, l. xxii, 5. Sept. 4. Aged sixty years.

730. **Susan Virginia Buch.** 2, l. ix, 4. Sept. 19. Aged six months.

731. **Margaret Keller,** m.n. Madden. 2, l. xxiii, 4. Dec. 5. Born Sept. 28, 1830, in Montour Co., Pa. Wife of Samuel E. Keller, of Lititz Mills.

732. **Laura Augusta Sturgis.** 2, l. x, 3. Dec. 16. Daughter of Charles and Emeline Sturgis. Aged five years.

733. **Peter Fielis.** 3, l. xxiii, 10. Dec. 26. Born in Düsseldorf, Rhenish Prussia, Oct. 23, 1783. Widower.

734. **John Maurice Albright.** 3, l. x, 15. Dec. 28. Son of Reuben Albright. Aged nearly three years.

1862.

735. **Margaret Clementine de Schweinitz.** 2, l. ix, 2. Feb. 14. Infant daughter of the Rev. Edmund de Schweinitz.

736. **John Metzgar.** 3, l. x, 16. Feb. 16. Aged three years.

737. **Jacob Rudy.** 3, l. xxiii, 11. Feb. 20. Born in Lititz, Oct. 12, 1796. A widower. Son of Christian Rudy.

738. **Levi Hull.** 3, l. xxiii, 12. March 1. The physician of the town, aged forty-nine years.

739. **Elizabeth Leinbach.** 2, l. xv, 15. April 24. Unmarried Sister. Born in Graceham, Md., Sept. 5, 1783.

740. **Maria Kendrick.** 2, l. xv, 14. May 20. Unmarried Sister. Born near Lancaster, June 2, 1799.

741a. **John Martin Beck** (third). 1, r. ix, 15. May 23. Unmarried. Born Nov. 8, 1838, a son of John and Johanna Augusta (Reinke) Beck.

A mechanical draughtsman in Bement's Industrial Works, Philadelphia. Died of consumption.

741b. **Beatus Evans.** Infant son of John Evans. July 12. 3, l. ix, 1.

742. **George Edward Keller.** 3, l. viii, 1. July 26. Infant.

743. **Aurelius Christ.** 3, l. ix, 2. July 27. Son of Augustus Christ. Aged two years.

744. **Olivia Loretta Kryder,** m.n. Rauch. 2, l. xxi, 16. July 27. Wife of Charles H. Kryder. Daughter of Henry Gottfried Rauch. She died suddenly within ten minutes of the death of her nephew (the foregoing), who expired while sitting on her lap.

745. **Samuel Alexander Diehm.** 3, l. viii, 2. July 29. Infant.

746. **Louisa Eichler.** 2, l. xvi, 13. Aug. 9. Unmarried Sister. Aged seventy-five years.

747. **Catharine A. Kraemer.** 2, l. xxi, 15. Nov. 22. Born in Lancaster, Feb. 1, 1775. Wife of John Kraemer.

748. **Charles William Kling.** 3, l. ix, 3. Nov. 28. Infant son of Jacob Kling.

749. **Herbert Benjamin Regennas.** 3, l. viii, 3. Nov. 30. Aged five years.

1863.

750. **Anna Maria Heiserman.** 2, l. x, 2. Feb. 22. Infant daughter of George Heiserman.

751. **John William Rauch.** 3, l. xxiii, 13. March 11. Born in Lititz, Aug. 18, 1790; a son of John Henry and Anna Christina (Stohler) Rauch. In 1814 he married Barbara Rudy, who died in 1825. His second wife was Anna Rosina Busse, of Nazareth, and his third union was with the widow Lucetta (Ritter) Wolle. Five children in the first marriage, two in the second. A confectioner and baker; in the latter line he was the first maker, here, of bretzels. He served the congregation as a member of the *Aufseher Collegium* and as a Trustee; and for the larger part of his life was prominent in church-music as a tenor singer, trombonist (soprano), and first violinist. Remembrance, yet unfaded, remains to many, of the fine old gentleman, in his drooping cloak, with his handsome ivory-rimmed violin under his arm, on his way to play in lovefeast. A real poet, he touched his lyre often to enhance the interest of a festal occasion, to comfort the mourner, and to make happier by his beautiful lines the young bridal couple.

752. **Eleanora Kreiter,** m.n. McCan. 2, l. xxi, 14. March 27. Born in Middletown, Pa., 1788. Non-Moravian.

753. **Ernestina Louisa Regennas.** 2, l. ix, 3. Infant daughter of Peter Regennas. Three years, six months.

754. **Mary Jane Reichel,** m.n. Gray. 2, l. xxi, 13. May 27. Born in Camden Valley, N. Y., May 10, 1832. Wife of the Rev. William C. Reichel, Principal of Linden Hall Seminary.

755. **Andrew Philip Grosh.** 3, l. xxiii, 14. Aug. 16. Born in Hempfield Township, Nov. 29, 1805. A son of Peter Grosh and Maria Catharina, m.n. Conrad. Served in the 179th Penna. Regiment in the Civil War.

1864.

756. **Christina Caroline Heiserman.** 2, l. x, 1. Jan. 6. Infant daughter of George Heiserman.
757. **George Lewis Frederick.** 3, l. xxiii, 15. Feb. 7. Born Nov. 26, 1826. Died from injuries resulting from a fall from the roof of the hotel at Wabank, on the Conestoga, incidental to its removal by Samuel Lichtenthaeler to Lititz.
758. **Thomas Lewis Frederick.** 3, l. ix, 4. Feb. 9. Son of the foregoing. Aged one year, nine months.
759. **George Lewis Frederick.** 3, l. viii, 4. Feb. 27. Son of George and Susanna (Murr) Frederick. Aged one year. A different family from the preceding one.
760. **Horace Rudolph Souder.** 3, l. ix, 5. March 1. Infant son of Daniel Souder.
761. **Thomas Franklin Diehm.** 3, l. viii, 5. March 1. Infant.
762. **Theodore J. Burnett.** 3, l. xxiii, 16. March 8. Born at Stroudsburg, Pa., June 4, 1820. Died in Harrisburg.
763. **Adam Kling.** 3, l. ix, 6. March 20. Child of Frederick Kling. Aged three years, four months.
764. **Clara Olivia Groff.** 2, l. ix, 1. April 10. Infant daughter of Martin and Adelaide (Kryder) Groff.
765. **Anna Rebecca Witmeyer.** 2, l. xxi, 12. July 26. Wife of Richard Witmeyer. Aged twenty-six years.
766. **Mary Elizabeth Keller.** 2, l. viii, 16. Aug. 14. Infant daughter of Edward and Maria Keller.
767. **Samuel Harvey Kreiter.** 3, l. viii, 6. Oct. 5. Son of Martin Kreiter. Aged six years.

1865.

768. **Adelaide Clementina Groff.** 2, l. xxi, 11. Jan. 15. Born in Warwick, Aug. 1, 1835. A daughter of Charles Henry and Olivia (Rauch) Kreiter. Married Martin S. Groff. They had one child, a daughter, that lived only one year. Before her marriage she was a teacher of music in the Bordentown, N. J., Young Ladies' Seminary. Died of consumption.
769. **Rosina Klingman.** 2, l. xv, 13. Jan. 17. Born in Ischabrunn, Baden, Jan. 10, 1843. Daughter of Christopher and Barbara Klingman.
770. **James Munroe Derr.** 3, l. ix, 7. Jan. 23. Born in Lititz, Dec. 26, 1855, a son of Dr. John William and Juliana Derr. He was a hearty, active and very lively boy until shortly before his last Christmas.
771. **George Francis Haughman.** 3, l. viii, 7. Feb. 27. Infant son of George Washington and Amanda (Delbo) Haughman.
772. **Jacob Geitner.** 3, l. xxii, 1. March 5. Born Sept. 6, 1791. Son of John George Geitner, second. Married Joanna Elizabeth Beck. By trade a tanner. For thirty years a member of the *Aufseher Collegium*. Though somewhat taciturn and slow of speech, he was a man of excellent understanding, and a keen debater; his few words went usually straight to the truth of a discussion.

773. **John Stark.** 3, l. xvi, 7. April 6. Born Jan. 15, 1838. Unmarried. Son of Charles and Elizabeth Stark, of Warwick. He sustained an excellent character and was a great help to his parents. On the 4th of April he met with an accident on the railroad, which resulted in his death.

774. **Laura Susanna Schmidt.** 2, l. vii, 16. May 10. Born Jan. 24, 1863. Daughter of John and Amelia Louisa (Regennas) Schmidt. Diphtheria.

775. **Susanna Elizabeth Bachman.** 2, l. xxi, 10. June 23. Born in Lititz, Nov. 2, 1778, a daughter of Andrew and Elizabeth Albright. Was married to the widower John Philip Bachman, Dec. 19, 1800. She lived to see 26 grandchildren, and eleven great-grandchildren.

776. **William Demuth Kreider.** 3, l. ix, 8. July 16. Infant son of William Eugene and Mary Josephine (Demuth) Kreider.

777. **Mary Elizabeth Seaber.** 2, l. viii, 15. Aug. 3. Infant daughter of Henry and Mary Elizabeth (Sturgis) Seaber.

778. **Haydn Albert Habecker.** 3, l. viii, 8. Sept. 10. Infant son of Isaac and Rebecca (Reidenbach) Habecker.

779. **Helen Beck.** 2, l. vii, 15. Sept. 24. Daughter of Abraham Reinke and Joanna Salome (Huebener) Beck. Aged fifteen months.

780. **Catharine Tshudy.** 2, l. xxi, 9. Oct. 23. She was born Nov. 4, 1775, in York County, a daughter of Jacob and Elizabeth Blickensderfer. Moved to Lititz when fourteen years of age, and became a communicant member of the congregation. In 1798 she was married to Matthias Gottfried Tshudy. They had one son and five daughters. She became blind about a year and a half before her end.

1866.

781. **William Grant Seaber.** 3, l. ix, 9. Jan. 12. Infant son of Christian Samuel and Lydia Ann Seaber.

782. **Beata Schmidt.** 2, l. viii, 14. Jan. 20. A twin child of John Schmidt.

783. **Emma Ernestina Rickert.** 2, l. xxii, 4. Feb. 7. She was born in Bethania, N. C., Aug. 26, 1820; a daughter of Bishop Peter Wolle and his wife Maria Theresa, m.n. Shober. She was married to Ferdinand Daniel Rickert, in 1845. Was afflicted with epilepsy nearly all her life, and died suddenly.

784. **Elizabeth Keller,** m.n. Erb. 2, l. xxiii, 3. Feb. 18. Born in 1792. Wife of Samuel Keller, of Lititz Mills.

785. **Elmer Stauffer Kauffman.** 3, l. viii, 9. Feb. 25. Infant son of Emmanuel Kauffman.

786. **Joanna Elizabeth Geitner.** 2, l. xxii, 3. March 8. Born in Graceham, Md., May 31, 1796; a daughter of the Rev. John Martin Beck and his wife, Anna Johanna, m.n. Grubé. Wife of Jacob Geitner. She had seven children, of whom three survived her.

787. **Beata Enck.** 2, l. vii, 14. March 23. Franklin Enck's child.

788. **Laura Augusta Keller.** 2, l. viii, 13. April 11. Daughter of Edward Keller. One year, five months.

789. **Beatus Kreiter.** 3, l. ix, 10. July 7. Son of Charles W. Kreiter.

790. **Beata Kreiter.** 2, l. vii, 13. Nov. 6. Child of Aurora Kreiter, of Warwick.

791. **Jacob Blickensderfer Tshudy.** 3, l. xxi, 1. Nov. 8. He was born in Lititz, Nov. 30, 1805; a son of Matthias Gottfried Tshudy. From his tenth to his fourteenth year he was a pupil in Nazareth Hall. In 1828 he married Joanna Caroline Levering, who died in 1830. His second wife was Caroline Harbaugh, with whom he had two sons and two daughters. In 1828 he opened a general store, here, and was very successful in business. He held a number of honorable and trustworthy offices, and was widely known and highly esteemed throughout Lancaster County. For many years he enriched our Church-music with his good tenor voice, and was also one of the violinists.

792. **Christian Henry Rauch.** 3, l. xxii, 2. Nov. 22. Born in Lititz, July 19, 1788; a son of John Henry and Anna Christina (Stohler) Rauch. Married his first wife (m.n. Romig) in 1812. They had four sons and four daughters. His second wife, the widow Wickel, he married in 1850. His first occupation was that of a stocking-weaver; then he followed surveying and conveyancing, and from 1820 to 1860 he was a Justice of the Peace. As a musician he served the congregation with his violoncello and as a bass-singer and trombonist. He was all his life a steady reader, and fond of an occasional good novel. In 1810 he wrote a text-book on Arithmetic, *Des Deutschen Bauers und Landmanns Rechenbuch, und des Schullehrers Gehülfe;* printed in Easton by Christian Jacob Hütter. Candor was a distinguishing trait of his character.

793. **Beatus Heiserman.** Child of George Heiserman.

794. **Susanna Regennas.** 2, l. xxiii, 2. Dec. 5. Born in Lititz, Dec. 14, 1794. Daughter of Frederick Peter Kreiter. Wife of John Jacob Regennas.

1867.

795. **Beata Keller.** 2, l. viii, 12. March 6. Samuel E. Keller's child.

796. **Eliza Schnell.** 2, l. xvi, 12. March 12. Born in Reading, Pa., Oct. 17, 1809. Unmarried Sister. Afflicted with deafness for many years. A dressmaker.

797. **Salome Huebener.** 2, l. xxi, 8. May 25. She was born in Lititz, March 5, 1803; a daughter of Matthias Gottfried Tshudy. In the spring of 1823 she became a teacher in Linden Hall Seminary, and in October, of the same year, was married to the Rev. Samuel Renatus Huebener. With him she served in the congregations of Friedland, N. C., Gnadenhütten, Ohio, Graceham, Md., Friedberg, N. C., and Salem, N. C., where her husband departed suddenly, June 7, 1849; then she returned to Lititz, serving here as a Deaconess. She had nine children. The Rev. Lewis Renatus Huebener was one of her sons. For the praise that might be given her, she would not have wished.

798. **Lucetta Rauch,** m.n. Ritter. 2, l. xxii, 2. May 28. Born in Philadelphia, Feb. 22, 1804. Married S. Henry Wolle. They had three

sons and two daughters. Some years after her husband's death she became a teacher in Linden Hall Seminary, and served faithfully in that capacity for more than eighteen years. In 1859 she married the widower John William Rauch. Died of a cancer.

799. **Lucy Ann Roth,** m.n. Fielis. 2, l. xxi, 7. Aug. 17. Non-Moravian. Aged thirty-four years.

800. **Carrie Hortense Tshudy.** 2, l. vii, 12. Sept. 6. Infant daughter of Richard Rush Tshudy. Aged eleven months.

801. **Infant son of Obed Bowman.** 3, l. ix, 11. Sept. 17.

802. **James Edward Sturgis.** 3, l. viii, 11. Infant son of James and Eliza Sturgis.

803. **Samuel Lichtenthaeler.** 3, l. xxi, 2. Oct. 2, Born Feb. 3, 1808. In 1832 he married Catharine Kraemer. They had six children, two sons and four daughters. He was a son of Adolph Lichtenthaeler. For many years he carried on the business of cabinet-making here. About the year 1854 he purchased the Lititz Springs Hotel property, where, being of a genial disposition, kind-hearted and obliging, he— not to forget the capable assistance of his good wife and daughters —made a model landlord. Having much ability as an architect, he gave his valuable aid to the congregation in designing the Hotel building, the changes in Church and Parsonage, and the southern addition to Linden Hall. He designed also the Moravian Church in Lebanon, Pa.

804. **Infant son of Theodore Lichtenthaeler.** 3, l. ix, 12. Dec. 7.

805. **Martha Huber.** 2, l. viii, 11. Daughter of John Huber. Infant.

1868.

806. **Daniel Kreider.** 3 l. xxii, 3. Jan. 3. He was born March 22, 1799; a son of Frederick Peter and Catharine (Leinbach) Kreiter. In 1822 he married Maria Louisa Lennert, who died in 1836. They had six children, only two surviving their mother. In 1837 he married Anna Maria Meyers. Of this union there were two children, a boy and a girl, the former dying in his infancy. The mother died on the fourteenth anniversary of her marriage. His third marriage was to Jemima Leinbach. By trade, a saddler.

807. **Edward Grant Habecker.** 3, l. viii, 12. Feb. 9. One year.

809. **Alice Elizabeth Opitz.** 2, l. vii, 11. Feb. 22. Daughter of Catharine Diehm. Aged three years.

810. **Beata Lichtenthaeler.** 2, l. viii, 10. March 4. Daughter of Charles Lichtenthaeler.

811. **Maria Louisa Seaber.** 2, l. vii, 10. March 6. Infant daughter of Samuel and Lydia Seaber.

812. **Harriet Amelia Bowman.** 2, l. xxiii, 1. May 3. Wife of Obed Bowman. Aged thirty-nine years.

813. **Benjamin Kreiter.** 3, l. xxi, 3. May 12. Born in Lititz, June 20, 1786. A son of Peter Kreiter and his second wife Anna Maria, born Kohn. In 1810 he married Anna Maria Seyfried, of Nazareth, who died in 1824. By this marriage he had eight children. His

second wife was Eleanor Bandon, a widow; two children. He was not a member of the Congregation at the time of his death.

814. **Henry William Hall.** 3, l. xvi, 8. May 19. Born in Lititz, Sept. 9, 1809. A son of Christian Hall. Unmarried. Served as a teacher in Nazareth Hall, and in the Lititz Academy. Followed the business of clock-making, and for many years was organist of the Congregation. Not a church-member at the time of his decease.

816. **Jacob Rock.** 3, l. xxi, 4. June 7. He was born in Cocalico Township, Nov. 21, 1774. United with this congregation in 1800. Accompanied the Rev. Denke as Assistant to the Mission in New Fairfield, Canada. Married Susanna Magdalena Christ. They had seven children. In 1858 he moved to Marietta to live with his daughter, Cornelia; and later, with her, to Philadelphia, and then to Blair County. Having been seriously injured by a fall, whilst living in Marietta, he was confined to his room for the last nine years of his life. By trade a tailor.

817. **Susan Lavinia Habecker.** 2, l. viii, 9. July 31. Daughter of Isaac and Rebecca Habecker. Aged six years.

818. **Samuel Kreiter.** 3, l. xxii, 5. Aug. 27. He was born in Lititz, June 4, 1790; a son of Friederich Peter and Catharine (Leinbach) Kreiter. Married Elizabeth Westhaefer, April 20, 1817. By trade a cooper. He served as a soldier in the War of 1812.

819. **Edward Augustus Diehm.** 3, l. ix, 13. Aged two years.

820. **Charles Stark.** 3, l. xxi, 5. Oct. 15. Aged fifty-six years. Non-Moravian.

821. **Fredericka Louisa Lindenlos.** 2, l. xv, 12. Oct. 28. She was born in Amsterdam, June 10, 1793. Brought to America when she was about six years of age, and lived, first, with a Quaker family in Maryland, and later in York. Came to Lititz in 1815. Some mystery attaches to the circumstances which led to her coming to this country. Of her early childhood she had only a misty recollection; but she kept a distinct remembrance of a visit from a handsome, richly-dressed lady who gave her sweetmeats and wept over her; and there was a sea-faring man who, by his promise of some nice present, induced her to go with him to his ship. Whether she was thrown upon the world purposely, or kidnapped, this is certain, that her lines, subsequently, were cast in pleasant places, for here, with Samuel Sturgis' family, with the Petersens, and finally in the Sisters' House, she found a home, and everybody had a good word for old "Lindy."

1869.

822. **Beatus Russel.** 3, l. viii, 13. Jan. 12.

823. **Beata Sturgis.** 2, l. vii, 9. Jan. 15. Daughter of Nathan Sturgis.

824. **Anna Maria Kling,** m.n. Licht. 2, l. xxii, 1. Jan. 14. Born in Flacht, Würtemberg, Jan. 14, 1805. Wife of Adam Kling, of Warwick. Came to this country in 1854. Not a member of this congregation. Died suddenly of apoplexy.

825. **Catharine Holl,** m.n. Beck. 2, l. xxi, 5. Jan. 17. Born in New Holland, March 25, 1783. Came to Lititz in 1849, with her daughter, the widow Barr, with whom she lived upwards of thirty years.

826. **Martin Eck.** 3, l. xxii, 4. March 17. Born in Hesse-Darmstadt, in 1829. Served this country as a soldier in the Civil War. Not a member of the Congregation.

827. **George David Thomas.** 3, l. xxii, 6. April 25. He was born in Lancaster, Sept. 29, 1803; a son of George Thomas. He came to Lititz in his thirteenth year, after his father's death, and was apprenticed to Jacob Greider to learn shoemaking. Married Catharine Sheed, Jan. 3, 1826. They had one son and four daughters, of whom one daughter survived him. In the same year, in which he was married, he was appointed chief-sacristan of the congregation, and from that time, for forty-three years, attended to the duties imposed upon him by this office with much care and faithfulness.

828. **Emmanuel Holl.** 3, l. xxi, 6. July 27. Born April 20, 1844. Served in the army during the Civil War: first in the 122d Regiment, Co. F., P. V., for nine months; then in Nevin's Independent Battery, six months, and finally in the same until the end of the war. Married Catharine Diehm. Died of consumption.

829. **John Alexander Sturgis.** 3, l. ix, 14. Aug. 17. Infant son of James and Eliza Sturgis.

830. **Edward Price Seaber.** 3, l. viii, 14. Sept. 4. Infant son of Charles and Mary Seaber.

831. **Christian Gottlieb Oehme.** 3, l. xxii, 7. Dec. 5. Born Feb. 12, 1801; a son of John Erdman Oehme. Married Margaret Gernand. Lived in Lexington, near Lititz.

832. **Christian Frederick Youngman.** 3, l. xxi, 7. Dec. 5. He was born in Bethlehem, Sept. 6, 1810; a son of Peter Youngman. Married Rebecca Lennert. For thirty-six years he was the ticket agent, at Lancaster, of the Penna. R. R. Co., winning in that capacity the entire confidence of his official superiors and, because of his kindness and courtesy, that of the traveling public.

833. **Matilda Miksch.** 2, l. xxi, 4. Dec. 21. Born Sept. 21, 1821; a daughter of Samuel and Elizabeth Kreiter. Married to James H. Miksch, April 29, 1845.

1870.

834. **Bertha Frailey.** 2, l. viii, 8. June 20. Infant.

835. **Cora Virginia Grosh.** 2, l. vii, 8. March 1. Born April 7, 1865. Daughter of Samuel and Amanda Grosh. Died of scarlet fever.

836. **Haydn Hamet Albright.** 3, l. ix, 15. March 4. Son of Reuben Albright. Aged six years. Died of scarlet fever.

837. **Elizabeth Sophia Diehm.** 2, l. viii, 7. March 4. Daughter of Oliver Diehm. Aged nine years. Died of scarlet fever.

838. **Horace Linnaeus Weltmer.** 3, l. viii, 15. March 11. Son of Dr. Jonas Weltmer. One year, five months. Scarlet fever.

839. **Christoph Tschopp.** 3, l. xvi, 9. March 14. Unmarried. Born in Switzerland. Aged seventy-eight years. Non-Moravian. Died of consumption.

840. **Martha Ann Enck.** 2, l. vii, 7. March 26. Daughter of B. Franklin Enck. Died of scarlet fever, aged two years.

841. **Susan Amanda Seaber.** 2, l. viii, 6. April 16. Daughter of Samuel Seaber. Died of scarlet fever, aged three years and seven months.

842. **Della Elizabeth Delbo.** 2, l. vii, 6. April 22. Daughter of Darius Delbo. Died of scarlet fever, aged three years.

843. **William Albert Brenneman.** 3, l. ix, 16. April 28. Son of John Brenneman. Aged two years, seven months. Scarlet fever.

844. **Rosina Brunner.** 2, l. xvi, 11. May 17. Unmarried Sister. Born in Christianspring, near Nazareth, April 24, 1792. Came to Lititz in her seventeenth year. Lived nearly all her life in the Sisters' House, holding various official positions.

845. **Horace Grant Stark.** 3, l. viii, 16. May 20. Son of Samuel Stark. Aged one year, seven months. Scarlet fever.

846. **Adam Henry Habecker.** 3, l. vii, 1. June 18. Son of Isaac Habecker. Aged ten months. Consumption.

847. **Albert Henry Frailey.** 3, l. vi, 1. July 8. Son of Hiram Frailey. Died of scarlet fever, aged two years.

848. **Joseph Eschbach.** 3, l. xxii, 8. July 23. Born in Inlenheim, near Strasburg. Came to this country in 1854. Aged sixty-two years. Non-Moravian.

849. **Caroline Catharine Haughman.** 2, l. viii, 5. July 24. Infant daughter of George W. Haughman.

850. **Mahlon Shirk.** 3, l. vii, 2. July 29. Infant.

851. **Friedrich Wilhelm Kling.** 3, l. vi, 2. Aug. 2. Son of Frederick and Catharine (Herkel) Kling. Aged two months.

852. **Philip Conn.** 3, l. xxi, 8. Aug. 9. Born in Lancaster, June 23, 1793. Married at Emmaus, 1823, Sarah Ann Geitner. As "Pappy Conn" he was affectionately known to many Lititz Academy boys who boarded with him.

853. **Lilly Agnes Haughman.** 2, l. viii, 4. Born March 8, 1861. Died Aug. 25, 1861, in Petersburg; reinterred here Sept. 1870.

854. **Kate Landstreet Holl.** 2, l. vii, 5. Aug. 23. Infant daughter of Emmanuel Holl. Aged one year.

855. **Sophia Augusta Bricker.** 2, l. xv, 11. Aug. 30. Unmarried Sister. Born May 8, 1849; a daughter of David and Lucinda (Petersen) Bricker. She died, while on a visit to Lebanon, of typhoid fever.

856. **Bernhard Martin Tshudy.** 3, l. vii, 3. Sept. 5. Infant son of Haydn and Emma (Hull) Tshudy.

857. **Anna Maria Kreiter.** 2, l. xvi, 10. Oct. 21. Unmarried Sister. Born Oct. 8, 1824. A daughter of Benjamin and Anna Maria (Seyfried) Kreiter. Died of a cancer.

858. **Mary Jane Baker.** 2, l. xv, 10. Dec. 20. Aged twenty-two years. Non-Moravian.

859. **Harry Franklin Bollinger.** 3, l. vi, 3. Dec. 24. Infant son of William H. Bollinger.

1871.

860. **John Ricksecker.** 3, l. xxii, 9. Jan. 29. Born in Lititz, June 6, 1789. A son of John and Rachel (Frederick) Ricksecker. Married Louisa Fredericka Fisher. The latter part of his life he spent with his son in Mount Joy, where he died. Not a member of this congregation at the time of his death.

861. **Christiana Catharine Reidenbach,** m.n. Yerger. 2, l. xxi, 3. Aug. 31. Born June 27, 1848. Wife of Aaron Reidenbach.

862. **George Washington Broome Viven.** 3, l. xvi, 10. Nov. 7. Unmarried. Born in Philadelphia, Oct. 24, 1850. Age twenty-one years.

863. **Elizabeth Sturgis,** m.n. Shiffer. 2, l. xxi, 2. Nov. 26. Born in Mount Joy Township, 1848. Wife of Nathan O. Sturgis.

864. **Anna Rosina Rauch.** 2, l. xxi, 1. Dec. 7. Born in Bethlehem, Sept. 10, 1796. She was the widow of Henry Gottfried Rauch. Her maiden name was Kornmann. After her husband's death she kept the infant school for girls, here, for twelve years.

865. **Howard Jacob Tshudy.** 3, l. vii, 4. Dec. 10. Infant son of Richard Rush and Sarah Tshudy.

866. **Abraham B. Kreiter.** 3, l. vi, 4. Dec. 30. Child of G. W. Kreiter.

1872.

867. **Herman Darius Kling.** 3, l. vii, 5. Jan. 27. Son of Jacob Kling. Died of scarlet fever, aged one year, eight months.

868. **Della Augusta Stark.** 2, l. vii, 4. Feb. 2. Infant daughter of Samuel Stark. Died of scarlet fever, aged ten months.

869. **Helen Sophia Bachman.** 2, l. xvi, 9. Feb. 16. Unmarried Sister. Born in Lititz, Sept. 27, 1806; a daughter of John Philip Bachman, organ-builder. Her mother's maiden name was Albright. She was the sick-nurse in Linden Hall for twenty-five years. Deceased from an attack of apoplexy.

870. **Beata Albright.** 2, l. viii, 3. Feb. 23.

871. **Anna Sophia Roberts.** 2, l. xx, 16. March 13. Born in Lititz, Jan. 14, 1794; a daughter of Daniel and Anna Maria (Kleinmann) Christ. Married John Roberts of Marietta.

872. **Maurice Edwin Kreider.** 3, l. vi, 5. March 26. Son of Martin Kreider. Died of scarlet fever, aged two years.

873. **Magdalena Frederick,** m.n. Göttman. 2, l. xix, 16. April 9. Born in Gnadenthal, near Nazareth, Oct. 23, 1787. Moved hither with the second Steinman family. Married the widower Christian Frederick, who died in 1834. From 1835 she lived on Pine Hill.

874. **George Adam Kling.** 3, l. xxi, 9. May 7. Born March 24, 1803, in Flacht, Würtemberg. Married Anna Maria Licht. Came to America in 1854. Lived in Warwick. Lutheran.

875. **John Herman Kling.** 3, l. vii, 6. July 21. Infant son of Jacob Kling.

876. **Mary Ann Holl,** m.n. Whitcraft. 2, l. xx, 15. Aug. 7. Wife of Isaac Holl.

877. **Francis Lewis Lennert.** 3, l. xvi, 11. Aug. 10. Born in Lititz, Nov. 17, 1805. Unmarried. A son of John Peter and Joanna Susanna (Knauss) Lennert. Not a member of the Congregation at the time of his death. A clock and watchmaker. Played the serpent in the village music.

878. **William Nauman Bollinger.** 3, l. vi, 6. Aug. 13. Infant son of William H. Bollinger.

879. **Henry Richard Rickert.** 3, l. vii, 7. Sept. 2. Infant son of Richard Rickert.

880. **Carl Friedrich Kling.** 3, l. vi, 7. Sept. 19. Infant son of Friedrich and Catharine Kling.

881. **Edmund Samuel Grosh.** 3, l. vii, 8. Nov. 1. Son of Samuel and Amanda (Kraemer) Grosh. Died of membranous croup, aged five years.

882. **Abraham Van Vleck.** 3, l. xxii, 10. Nov. 21. Born in Lititz, June 15, 1784; a son of Henry Van Vleck (hatter) and his second wife, Elizabeth, m.n. Riem. Married twice, and had four children. Served as teacher in Nazareth Hall, in New York, and at Savannah, and finally settled in Newark, N. J. Returned to live in Lititz after an absence of fifty years.

883. **Eliza Adeline Michael.** 2, l. xv, 9. Dec. 23. Unmarried Sister. For many years a domestic in John Beck's family. Having become insane, she was removed to the Hospital, at Lancaster, where she died.

884. **Maria Louisa Hamm,** m.n. Dinges. 2, l. xx, 1. Dec. 24. She was born in Schnabenheim, Hesse Darmstadt, Aug. 16, 1794. United with the Moravians in Neuwied. Married Feb., 1823, to John Hamm, and came to this country in 1827. She had four sons and three daughters, six of whom died in their childhood. Died of dropsy.

885. **Frederick Adolphus Zitzman.** 3, l. xxi, 10. Dec. 24. Born in Amsterdam, June 7, 1787. Came to this country in his fifteenth year. Married Susanna Miller. He was the landlord of the Lititz Springs Hotel for two years. Appointed Postmaster, in Lititz, by President Andrew Jackson, and continued in this office nineteen years.

886. **Martha Ellen Seaber.** 2, l. vii, 3. Dec. 28. Daughter of Charles Seaber. Died of diphtheria and croup, aged nine years and nine months.

1873.

887. **Morris Herbert Seaber.** 3, l. vi, 8. Dec. 31. Son of Charles Seaber. Died of diphtheria and croup, aged six years.

888. **Anna Mary Bollinger.** 2, l. viii, 2. Jan. 29. Daughter of William H. Bollinger. Died of diphtheria, aged five years and ten months.

889. **John Beck.** 3, l. xxii, 11. February 11. He was born June 16, 1791, at Graceham, Md., where his parents, the Rev. John Martin and Anna Johanna (Grubé) Beck were then stationed. Having been educated in Nazareth Hall, he was sent to Lititz in 1805, and here was apprenticed to Gottfried Traeger with whom he served his time

6

as a shoemaker. In 1815 he was appointed to take charge of the village school for boys, from which humble beginning was evolved his famous Boarding School, the Lititz Academy—his own institution, not a church school—which was conducted by him, with great success and without personal or public solicitation, from 1819 until 1865. On the second of February, 1819, he married Joanna Augusta Reinke. At the Golden Anniversary of their wedding he gave a lovefeast, in the church, to the congregation and a dinner to his descendants and nearest friends at the Springs Hotel.

For his calling he was especially gifted; excelling as a teacher, it was a pleasure as well as an advantage to be taught by him, and to experience his influence for good was to many a boy a blessing. Of a cheerful disposition and a winning personality, simple-hearted and guileless, he had yet a remarkable sense of character, so that he could measure a boy almost as soon as he first saw him. Impartially faithful to his pupils, whether they were of high or low estate, bright or dull; scorning the use of sarcastic speech to a defenceless lad; readily giving his kind word of commendation when it was deserved, and bringing to the settlement of difficulties in discipline a superb degree of tact, he won the absolute confidence of his patrons and the lasting love of his boys. The whole number of his pupils during fifty years was 2326.

His activity, however, was not limited to his own educational routine: the public schools of the place and the adjacent country, the Sunday Schools here and elsewhere, claimed his attention always; and, ever appreciative of the beautiful, he planted, at his own expense, a great many of the trees that now yield their grateful shade in our Springs Park.

His long and useful life, through which he never failed to recognize his Heavenly Father's guidance, was perfectly rounded out by the voluntary assistance he gave, until within two weeks of his decease, in his son's private school for boys.

890. **Susan Sturgis.** 2, l. xx, 2. March 26. Born near York, Jan. 3, 1786; a daughter of Jacob and Susan Correll. Wife of Samuel Sturgis. She had fourteen children; sixty-one grandchildren, and eighty-two great-grandchildren.

891. **Caroline Tshudy,** m.n. Harbaugh. 2, l. xx, 3. April 3. Born at Graceham, Md., Sept. 18, 1808. She was the second wife of Jacob B. Tshudy.

892. **Edward Reuben Albright.** 3, l. vii, 9. June 25. Infant son of Reuben Albright.

893. **Jacob Correll Sturgis.** 3, l. xxi, 11. June 25. Born in Lititz, Oct. 13, 1808; a son of Samuel and Susan (Correll) Sturgis. Married Mary Ann Cassler. For about sixteen years he served the congregation as its sexton, and in earlier life was one of the trombonists. By trade a potter.

894. **Christianna Fredericka Essig,** born Kling. 2, l. xix, 1. July 12. Born in Flacht, Würtemberg, Feb. 10, 1832. Wife of Christian Frederick Essig.

895. **Susan Keller,** late Bard. 2, l. xix, 2. July 17. Born Dec. 31, 1836. Wife of Samuel E. Keller.

896. **Annie Caroline Stark.** 2, l. vii, 2. Aug. 25. Daughter of Henry and Susan Stark. Died of diphtheria, aged five years.

897. **Gustav Adolph Kreiter.** 3, l. xvi, 12. Sept. 15. A son of Benjamin Kreiter. Aged sixty-two years. Not a member of the congregation.

898. **Mary Ann Sturgis,** m.n. Cassler. 2, l. xix, 3. Nov. 24. Born near Nazareth, Sept. 8, 1813. Wife of Jacob Correll Sturgis. She had five sons and two daughters.

899. **Beata Sturgis.** 2, l. viii, 1. Dec. 27. Daughter of Julius F. Sturgis.

1874.

900. **Christian Kreiter.** 3, l. xxii, 12. Jan. 1. Born Jan. 3, 1789; a son of Christian and Regina Kreiter. Married Catharine Boehmer, who died in 1852. Died at Kissel Hill.

901. **Sarah Blenzinger,** late Stober. 2, l. xx, 4. Feb. 15. Born near Ephrata in 1802. Wife of David Blenzinger.

902. **Sarah White,** m.n. Diehm. 2, l. xix, 4. Feb. 17. Born in Lititz, Nov. 13, 1803. Divorced from her husband, William White, she lived for years with her brother, Jacob Diehm.

903. **Emilie Louisa Schmidt,** m.n. Regennas. 2, l. xix, 15. April 10. Born in Lititz, Aug. 7, 1833. Wife of John Schmidt.

904. **Anna Rebecca Enck.** 2, l. vii, 1. May 1. Daughter of Andrew and Mary Ann Enck, aged eleven years.

905. **Beata Regennas.** 2, l. vi, 16. June 3. Daughter of W. H. Regennas.

906. **John Jacob Seaber.** 3, l. xxi, 12. July 10. Born in Warwick, April 4, 1797. Married Susannah Knauss. Engaged in various pursuits, and was for many years proprietor of the daily stage-line between Lititz and Lancaster.

907. **Maria Elizabeth Friederich,** m.n. Steiger. 2, l. xx, 5. Sept. 9. Born in Germany, Aug. 16, 1813. Wife of John Leonhard Friederich. Died very suddenly, after having had repeated strokes of apoplexy.

908. **Joseph William Gochenaur.** 3, l. vi, 9. Sept. 14. Infant son of Albert and Thamar (Oehme) Gochenaur.

909. **Julia Antoinette Huebener.** 2, l. xvi, 8. Dec. 4. Born at Gnadenhütten, Ohio, Dec. 5, 1832; a daughter of the Rev. Samuel and Salome (Tshudy) Huebener. At about the age of two years she met with an accident which hindered her just development of mind and body. Unmarried Sister.

910. **Catharine Thomas.** 2, l. xix, 5. Dec. 27. She was born, in Philadelphia, June 7, 1797; a daughter of George William and Christiana Sheed. Baptized by Bishop White, in Christ Church. Three days after her birth her mother died; and after her father's death, in the following year, she was adopted by Samuel Grosh, of Lititz. For a time she served as a teacher in Linden Hall Seminary. Married to George David Thomas, Jan. 3, 1826.

1875.

911. **Julius Theodore Beckler.** 3, l. xxii, 13. March 8. Born June 26, 1814, at New Dorp, Staten Island, where his parents, the Rev. John Christian and Augusta Henrietta Beckler were then stationed. Educated in Nazareth Hall, and prepared for the ministry in the Theological Seminary at Nazareth, serving, later, as a professor in both institutions. In 1838 he married Emma Cornelia Smith, who died in 1853. He served in the pastorates of Bethania, N. C., and Emmaus, Pa.; and in 1846 was appointed Warden and assistant to the pastor in Lititz. On Oct. 12, 1854, he married Theodora Elizabeth Frueauff, and in the following year succeeded the Rev. Eugene Frueauff as Principal of Linden Hall Seminary, continuing in that position until June, 1862. During the impendence of civil war, and its first years of duration, the patronage of this school was, naturally, much diminished. Later he established a private school, here, for girls. Like his father, he was a good musician.

912. **Walter Lincoln Seaber.** 3, l. vii, 10. March 23. Infant son of Samuel and Lydia Seaber. Died suddenly, of croup, aged eight months.

913. **Rebecca Youngman.** 2, l. xx, 6. May 9. Born Sept. 22, 1793; a daughter of John Peter Lennert. Served eleven years as a teacher in Linden Hall Seminary. Married in 1822 to Christian Frederick Youngman, and lived here with him until 1835, when they moved to Lancaster. After her husband's death she came to live in Lititz.

914. **Maria Catharine Grosh,** m.n. Conrad. 2, l. xix, 6. June 13. Born in Berks County, April 14, 1782. Married Peter Grosh, with whom she lived first in Hempfield Township, then on one of the congregation farms near Lititz, and finally in Lititz. She had seven sons and three daughters; and lived to see thirty-eight grandchildren, one hundred and eighteen great-grandchildren, and thirteen great-great-grandchildren. Died unexpectedly, aged ninety-three years.

916. **David Eugene Frueauff.** 3, l. vi, 9. July 4. Born in Hollidaysburg, May 3, 1864; a son of John Frederick Frueauff. He died at the home of his father in Columbia. He was a very promising boy of pious inclination.

917. **Clinton Barton.** 3, l. vii, 11. July 21. Infant son of Elijah and Carrie (Reidenbach) Barton.

918. **Edith May Smith.** 2, l. vi, 15. Sept. 11. Infant daughter of George F. and Carrie (Sturgis) Smith.

919. **Amanda Regennas,** m.n. Wike. 2, l. xx, 7. Nov. 24. Born near Elizabeth Furnace, July 14, 1851. Wife of William Regennas. She died of consumption.

1876.

920. **Maria Christina Rauch,** m.n. Meyer. 2, l. xix, 7. April 9. Born at Heidelberg, Pa., Aug. 30, 1794. Married, first, to one of the name of Wickel, and in 1850 to the widower, Christian Henry Rauch.

921. **Martha Jane Reidenbach.** 2, l. vi, 14. June 8. Infant daughter of Aaron Reidenbach. Died of whooping cough.

922. **Daisy Irene Haughman.** 2, l. vi, 13. Infant daughter of G. W. Haughman. Died of marasmus.

923. **Elizabeth Michael.** 2, l. xx, 8. July 17. Born Dec. 21, 1790. Widow. She lived in the family of Samuel Seaber, who took care of her, she being a beneficiary of the congregation.

924. **Amanda Susan Bachman.** 2, l. xv, 8. Aug. 16. Unmarried Sister. Born in Lebanon Co., May 18, 1858; a daughter of Cornelius Bachman.

1877.

925. **Susanna Delbo,** m.n. Grosh. 2, l. xx, 9. Jan. 17. Born in Mechanicsville, Lancaster County, Dec. 25, 1801. Wife of Francis Delbo. Six children survived her.

926. **Elvina S. Keller,** m.n. Breitigam. 2, l. xix, 8. Jan. 25. Born in Reamstown, Oct. 6, 1835. A daughter of Benjamin Breitigam, and wife of Samuel E. Keller.

927. **Johanna Augusta Beck.** 2, l. xix, 9. March 28. She was born in Hope, N. J., Dec. 14, 1795; a daughter of the Rev. Abraham and Maria Sophia Reinke. In 1803 she was a pupil, and in 1816 a teacher in Linden Hall Seminary, serving in that capacity until Feb. 2, 1819, when she was married to John Beck. After her husband's death, in 1873, she left the old homestead and went to live with her son Abraham's family, where she passed the remainder of her fleeting days in serenity and pious meditation. A true Christian, of good mind and refined perceptions, she was not only a loving wife and mother, but the wise counselor and sympathetic confidant of her husband and children.

928. **Percy Monroe Flory.** 3, l. vi, 11. April 21. A son of Dallas and Frances (Sturgis) Flory, aged two years. Died of scarlet fever.

929. **Matilda M. Sohl.** 2, l. xx, 14. July 6. Born March 1, 1825; a daughter of Peter Fielis. Wife of Nathan Sohl.

930. **Ella S. Stark.** 2, l. xix, 14. Sept. 19. Born Sept. 14, 1848. Wife of Martin N. Stark.

931. **William Howard Greider.** 3, l. vii, 12. Sept. 22. A child of James Greider. Died of diphtheria, aged two years.

932. **Abraham Long.** 3, l. xxi, 13. Nov. 4. Born April 17, 1845, in West Hempfield Township. Died of consumption.

933. **Ella Augusta Seaber.** 2, l. vi, 12. Nov. 9. Infant daughter of Henry and Mary (Sturgis) Seaber.

934. **Juliana Greider.** 2, l. xx, 13. Dec. 3. She was born in Lititz, Nov. 21, 1791; a daughter of Daniel Christ. Served as a teacher in Linden Hall, and was a member of the church-choir. In 1814 she was married to Jacob Greider. Died of pneumonia.

1878.

936. **Susanna Seaber.** 2, l. xix, 13. Feb. 5. Born in Rittersville, Pa., April 21, 1795; a daughter of John and Mary (Wuensche) Knauss. In 1812 she came to Lititz and lived for several years in the family of her uncle, Adolph Lichtenthaeler. In 1820 she married Jacob

Seaber, with whom she located in Warwick, residing there for the remainder of her life. On May 18, 1870, they celebrated their Golden Wedding.

937. **Elizabeth Shreiber.** 2, l. xx, 12. June 9. Born in 1826, in Würtemberg, Germany. Non-Moravian.

938. **Richard Rush Tshudy.** 3, l. xx, 14. June 9. Born in Lititz, Feb. 18, 1835; a son of Jacob B. and Caroline Tshudy. Educated in John Beck's Academy and at Nazareth Hall. From 1853 to 1856 he was employed as a civil engineer on two railroads in the West, under the superintendence of Judge Jacob Blickensderfer. He married Sarah Catharine Hull. At the time of his death he was a Justice of the Peace. As a musician—violinist—he was an active member of the Lititz Philharmonic Society. A sociable and generous man, he was well liked by those who knew him best.

939. **Barbara Mumma Enck,** m.n. Lockard. 2, l. xviii, 1. July 8. Born Aug. 11, 1849. Wife of William Enck.

940. **Christian Bressner.** 3, l. xvi, 13. July 13. A stranger to Lititz. Served the Springs Hotel and two private gentlemen as hostler. As he was taking Dr. Shenk's horse to water a sudden movement of the animal cast him to the ground, death resulting soon afterward. No one appearing to claim the body, the Trustees of the Congregation granted it the privilege of interment here.

941. **Emma Ellen Oehme.** 2, l. xvi, 7. July 17. Born in Lititz, Dec. 27, 1859; a daughter of William Oehme.

942. **Clara Lavinia Hacker.** 2, l. vi, 11. Aug. 4. Infant.

943. **Helen Catharine Tshudy.** 2, l. vi, 10. Aug. 4. Infant daughter of Haydn H. and Emma (Hull) Tshudy.

944. **Laura Augusta Geitner.** 2, l. xv, 7. Aug. 29. Born in Lititz, Jan. 27, 1857; a daughter of Clement Geitner. Died of typhoid fever.

945. **Francis Delbo.** 3, l. xxii, 15. Sept. 12. Born at Chestnut Hill, Lancaster Co., Dec. 26, 1806. Married Susanna Grosh.

946. **Louisa Sophia Demmy,** m.n. Goethman. 2, l. xviii, 2. Nov. 25. Wife of Louis Demmy. Died of consumption, aged sixty years.

947. **Maria Elizabeth Hall.** 2, l. xvi, 6. Dec. 18. Born in the hotel at Lititz, of which her father, Christian Hall, was at that time landlord for the congregation, Feb. 2, 1818. In 1856 she moved into the Sisters' House where she ended her days.

1879.

949. **Laura Jeanette Lichtenthaeler.** 2, l. vi, 9. March 6. Daughter of Charles Lichtenthaeler. Died in Reading, aged six years.

950. **Willis Rickert.** 3, l. vii, 13. April 8. Infant son of Richard Rickert.

951. **Beatus Oehme.** 3, l. vi, 13. April 30. Child of H. L. Oehme.

952. **Charles Sands Zentmeyer.** 3, l. xvi, 14. Aug. 16. Born June 25, 1855; a son of Benjamin and Caroline (Sands) Zentmeyer. Unmarried.

953. **Ellen Yerger.** 2, l. vi, 8. Oct. 17. Daughter of John and Selina Yerger. Died of diphtheria and croup, aged seven years.

954. **Alice Yerger.** 2, 1. vi, 8. Oct. 21. Died of diphtheria, aged seven years. Twin sister of the foregoing.

955. **Katie Yerger.** 2, 1. vi, 7. Oct. 25. Daughter of Christian Yerger. Aged three years.

956. **Susan Yerger.** 2, 1. vi, 6. Oct. 30. Daughter of Christian Yerger. Aged one year, nine months.

957. **Elizabeth Yerger.** 2, 1. vi, 6. Oct. 31. Sister of the foregoing. Aged seven years.

958. **Maurice Edgar Rickert.** 3, 1. vii, 14. Nov. 17. Son of Charles Rickert. Aged two years.

959. **Augusta Fry.** 2, 1. vi, 5. Nov. 30. Child of Hiram and Sarah (Enck) Fry. Aged three years.

960. **Susanna Zitzman.** 2, 1. xviii, 3. Dec. 7. Born in the village of Rome, near Lititz, Nov. 21, 1790. Her parents were John and Elizabeth Miller. She was one of the first pupils of Linden Hall, and for a number of years taught music there. Married Frederick A. Zitzman. They celebrated their Golden Wedding in 1871. One son and two daughters survived her.

961. **Florence Stark.** 2, 1. vi, 4. Dec. 9. Daughter of Martin Stark. Aged nine years.

1880.

962. **Sarah Sturgis.** 2, 1. xviii, 4. Feb. 11. Born in the vicinity of Lititz, June 12, 1799; a daughter of Henry Rudy. Second wife of Alexander Sturgis.

963. **William Justus Furlow.** 3, 1. vi, 14. March 19. Child of Andrew Furlow.

964. **Edward George Grosh.** 3, 1. vii, 15. April 1. Child of Harrison H. Grosh. Playing with fire, his clothes igniting, terrible burns about his body caused his death after nearly two weeks of suffering. Aged three years, ten months.

965. **Jacob Henry Rickert.** 3, 1. xxii, 16. April 26. Born in Warwick, Sept. 12, 1809; a son of Daniel Rickert. Married Sophia Grosh; they had two sons. Toward the close of his life his mind weakened and it was found necessary to place him in the Lancaster Insane Asylum where he staid five months. Taken very sick there, he was brought home, dying soon afterward. By trade a blacksmith.

966. **Joseph Henry Sturgis.** 3, 1. vi, 15. May 7. Child of Nathan O. Sturgis.

967. **Florence Matilda Miksch.** 2, 1. xv, 6. May 20. Born March 21, 1865; a daughter of James H. and Matilda (Kreiter) Miksch.

968. **John C. Brickenstein.** 3, 1. xxi, 16. June 19. He was born Feb. 19, 1800, in the city of Basle, Switzerland, where his father was the pastor of a Moravian congregation. His early education was received from private teachers, mainly from an aunt. Having completed a classical course at Nisky, he studied in the Theological Seminary of Gnadenfeld, and then was called to America to be a teacher in Nazareth Hall, where he staid until 1830, acting also as one of the professors to three successive classes in the Theological

Seminary. In that year he received an appointment as pastor of the congregation at Emmaus, and was married to Anna Sophia Albright. From 1835 he served the Nazareth congregation for two years, and then filled a like position in Bethlehem until 1850. After a residence of four years on a farm in Middlesex Co., Va., he removed to Nazareth. Here he gave instruction in the classical languages and French in Nazareth Hall, and also lectured on Church History to the theological class then occupying the Whitefield House. In May, 1880, he came to Lititz to live with his son Hermann, Principal at that time of Linden Hall Seminary, and there he departed. He was a man of brilliant, scholarly attainments, and an exceptionally efficient teacher.

969. **General John Augustus Sutter.** Entombed in the north-west corner of the graveyard. He was born in Kandern, Baden, Feb. 15, 1803. Graduated at the military school in Berne, Switzerland. Went to France and joined the army of Charles X. About 1830, he came to America and settled in the western part of Missouri. In 1837 he removed to New Mexico and established himself in Santa Fe; then to California, settling there on the banks of the Sacramento River, and founding a colony named by him New Helvetia. From the Mexican government he received 100,000 acres of land for services rendered, but lost the whole of it through the indifference of Congress toward his claims resulting from the annexation of California. In 1847 gold was discovered on his ranch in that state. In 1871 he came to live in Lititz and from here went often to Washington to urge his just claims, but always to be disappointed. Having paid to the State of California $30,000 in taxes on the land of which he was bereft, that State granted him a pension of $3,000 a year; but his ideas of right and wrong were so strict that after ten years, when he had had returned to him the former sum, he refused to accept the latter any longer. He died in Washington, D. C., June 18, 1880, aged seventy-seven years. Although he was not a member of this congregation the Church was proud to give him a resting-place in its burial-ground. Some fifty of his fellow-pioneers came to his funeral, and among them were Generals John C. Fremont and H. T. Gibson, both of whom addressed the multitude of people gathered about the grave. Here he was known as a fine-looking, courtly old gentleman, and, because of his urbane and hospitable ways, was esteemed and respected by the whole community.

970. **Charles Edward Shultz.** 3, l. vii, 16. July 3. Infant son of the Rev. C. B. Shultz.

971. **Jennie Augusta Uhland.** 2, l. vi, 3. July 25.

973. **Maria Rosanna Kreiter.** 2, l. xvi, 5. Aug. 3. Born in 1809. A daughter of Michael C. Kreiter. Aged seventy-one years.

974. **Beatus Becker.** 3, l. vi, 16.

975. **Harry Firestone.** 3, l. v, 1. Sept. 11. Infant.

976. **Catharine Hull,** m.n. Kauffman. 2, l. xviii, 5. Sept. 13. She was born in East Hempfield Township, Feb. 5, 1817. Came in her child-

hood to Lititz, her father having been engaged to conduct the congregation inn. Educated in Linden Hall. Married to Dr. Levi Hull in 1836. Of twelve children she was survived by two sons and four daughters.

977. **Agnes Margaret Haisch.** 2, l. v, 16. Oct. 3. Daughter of Frederick Haisch. Died of diphtheria, aged six years.

978. **Herman Samuel Haisch.** 3, l. v, 2. Oct .4. Brother of the foregoing. Died of diphtheria, aged three years.

979. **Charles Augustus Flory.** 3, l. v, 3. Oct. 27. Child of Dallas Flory. Aged three years.

980. **John Hershey Baer.** 3, l. xx, 2. Born near Rohrerstown, Lancaster Co., Aug. 2, 1818; a son of Henry and Anna (Hershey) Baer. Married Barbara A. Minnich. Aged sixty-two years.

981. **Anna Maria Keller.** 2, l. xx, 11. Dec. 14. Born in Plainfield Township, Northampton Co., Feb. 5, 1828; a daughter of Henry and Lisetta Wolle. Came to Lititz in 1845 and carried on mantua-making until 1853, when she was appointed a teacher in the local Public School. In 1860 she was married to the widower George Edward Keller. Died of a cancer.

982. **Rose Cornelia Stewart.** 2, l. vi, 2. Dec. 25. Daughter of Thomas J. Stewart and Ellen, m.n. Shelley. Aged seven years.

1881.

983. **Edna Elizabeth Fry.** 2, l. vi, 1. Jan. 1. Child of Nathan C. Fry. Died of pneumonia, aged nine months.

984. **Susanna Catharine Regennas.** 2, l. xv, 5. Jan. 3. Born in 1823. Unmarried Sister. Aged fifty-seven years.

985. **Anna Sutter,** m.n. Dübeld. Entombed in the north-west corner of the graveyard. Born in Burgdorf, Switzerland, Sept. 15, 1806. Wife of General John A. Sutter. Three of her children survived her.

986. **Horace Becker Hull.** 3, l. xvi, 15. March 21. Born in Lititz, Feb. 20, 1856. Educated in the local Public School, Lititz Academy, and Nazareth Hall successively. A printer in the offices of the *Lancaster Inquirer* and the *Columbia Spy*. Unmarried.

987. **Robert Henry Grosh.** 3, l. v, 4. April 7. Son of Harrison Grosh. Aged nine years. Diphtheria and croup.

988. **Paul Eugene Seaber.** 3, l. v, 5. April 24. Son of Henry and Mary Seaber. Aged two years.

989. **Elizabeth Grace Regennas.** 2, l. v, 15. June 7. Child of William Regennas. One year old.

990. **John Garfield Beck.** 3, l. v, 6. June 18. Child of John and Anna Beck. Infant.

991. **Robert Walker Geitner.** 3, l. xvi, 16. June 18. Born in Lititz, Jan. 28, 1859; a son of Clement Geitner. Unmarried.

992. **Charles Adam Kling.** 3, l. v, 7. July 15. Child of Christian Kling. Died of whooping cough.

993. **Ellen Susan Sturgis.** 3, l. xvi, 4. July 30. Daughter of Henry Sturgis. Aged nearly fourteen years.

994. **Georgianna Ricksecker,** m.n. Breitigam. 2, l. xx, 10. Aug. 3. Born in Mount Joy, Jan. 7, 1846. Wife of John Tyler Ricksecker.

995. **Laura Regennas.** 2, l. v, 15. Aug. 14. Infant daughter of William Regennas.

997. **John Frederick Fett.** 3, l. xx, 3. Sept. 9. He was born in Heroldsberg, near Nuremberg, Bavaria, Aug. 4, 1800. Having been educated in the parish school he accepted a position in a mercantile house, but found it uncongenial to his tastes. Then, after four years of service as a clerk in the local magistrate's office, he entered the University of Erlangen in 1821, finished his studies in law, there, in 1824, and practiced his profession afterwards, very successfully, for six years in Nuremberg. Spiritually awakened by intercourse with one of the Brethren, a missionary of the Diaspora, he determined to devote his life to the service of the Church; and, closing his office in Nuremberg, he re-entered the university to study theology. After teaching in the schools of Gnadau and Neuwied, and engaging in pastoral and missionary labors in Basle, he accepted an appointment to enter the newly-organized Home Mission activity of our Church in this country. He was the first Home Missionary in our Province, his initial station being Philadelphia. In 1849 he was sent to Green Bay, Wisconsin, where he founded a flourishing congregation, but in consequence of increasing deafness was obliged to retire from that and other active service in 1863. In 1851 he had married Adeline Maria Greider, of Lititz, and to this place they now retired.

998. **Emma Salome Huebener.** 2, l. v, 14. Sept. 20. Daughter of Dr. Obadiah T. and Martha (Greider) Huebener, of Lancaster. Died of membraneous croup, aged four years.

999. **Mary Margaret Conrad.** 2, l. xv, 4. Nov. 8. Daughter of George and Catherine (Oehme) Conrad. Born in Lexington, near Lititz. Unmarried. Died in Lancaster, of typhoid pneumonia, aged nearly twenty years.

1000. **Eliza Susanna Diehm.** 2, l. xix, 12. Dec. 7. Born in Warwick, Aug. 12, 1821. Wife of William Diehm. In 1875 she was afflicted with paralysis from which she never entirely recovered. Much appreciated as a faithful sick-nurse.

1882.

1001. **Alice Adella Kreider.** 2, l. v, 13. Dec. 31. Infant daughter of Albert Kreider.

1002. **Lucinda Amelia Bricker.** 2, l. xix, 11. Jan. 1. Born in Lititz, March 29, 1816; a daughter of John and Rachel Petersen. In 1839 she was married to David Bricker. She served as a deaconess, her field of duty being among the Married Sisters.

1003. **Laura Augusta Seaber.** 2, l. xvi, 3. Jan. 4. Daughter of Charles Seaber. Died of typhoid fever, aged twenty-two years.

1004. **Temple Fielis Roth.** 3, l. v, 9. Jan. 23. Child of Horace Roth.

1005. **Louis Demmy.** 3, l. xx, 4. Died at Pine Hill, Feb. 10, aged sixty-seven years. His wife's maiden name was Louisa Sophia Frederick.

1006. **Sophia Rickert.** 2, 1. xix, 10. Feb. 16. Born near Petersburg, Lancaster County, Jan. 20, 1810; a daughter of Peter and Catharine Grosh. Married Henry Rickert.

1007. **Timothy Grosh.** 3, 1. xx, 5. March 2. Born near Petersburg, Aug. 21, 1808. A son of Peter Grosh. Twice married; the second time to Catharine Hermes.

1008. **Susan Stauffer.** 2, 1. xv, 3. March 9. Unmarried Sister. Born at Silver Spring, Lancaster County, Nov. 16, 1842; a daughter of Henry and Elizabeth (Eshelman) Stauffer. Died of consumption.

1009. **Gertrude S. Doster.** 2, 1. xvi, 2. July 8. Child of Henry K. and Lydia Doster. Aged nearly twelve years.

1010. **Charles Augustus Grosh.** 3, 1. xx, 6. July 21. Born in East Hempfield Township, this county, Aug. 17, 1802; a son of Peter and Catharine (Conrad) Grosh. Settled in Lititz in pursuit of his trade, which was that of blacksmith. In 1826 he married Susanna Shober. For thirty-eight years, as a sacristan of the church, he prepared the coffee on lovefeast days and for the trombonists on Easter mornings. In 1876 he and his wife celebrated their Golden Wedding.

1011. **Edith May Buch.** 2, 1. v, 12. Sept. 16. Infant daughter of J. Frank Buch.

1012. **Elizabeth Bricker.** 2, 1. xviii, 16. Oct. 26. A daughter of Peter Fielis. Married Samuel S. Bricker. Aged sixty-nine years.

1013. **Maria Louisa Henrietta Bosse.** 2, 1. xv, 2. Nov. 13. Unmarried Sister. She was born in Heerte, Duchy of Braunschweig, May 16, 1814. In 1849 she emigrated to America, and here took service, for several years, in the family of the Rev. Robert de Schweinitz at Graceham, Md., and in Lancaster. Later she found employment in the laundry of Linden Hall Seminary.

1014. **Daisy Irene Sturgis.** 2, 1. v, 11. Nov. 18. A child of Nathan O. Sturgis. Died of scarlet fever, aged one year.

1015. **Beatus Enck.** 3, 1. v, 10. Son of Frank Enck.

1016. **Augustus Justinus Sturgis.** 3, 1. xx, 7. Dec. 20. Born in Lititz, Nov. 12, 1815; a son of Samuel Sturgis. By trade a potter; also followed farming, near Lititz, and butchering. Married the widow Fanny Weber, m.n. Brubacher. In pursuance of his duty as overseer of the Springs park, while chopping up a tree which had fallen, he contracted a severe cold and then pneumonia, the cause of his death.

1017. **Jacob Diehm.** 3, 1. xx, 8. Dec. 28. Born on the Lititz Farm, Aug. 1, 1798; a son of Philip and Mary Diehm. For thirty-eight years he operated a distillery at Rome, near here, but passed the last nine years of his life in Lititz. Married Sophia Bricker, with whom he celebrated a Golden Wedding in 1875.

1883.

1018. **Annie Maria Cable.** 2, 1. v, 10. Jan. 13.

1019. **Catharine Grosh,** m.n. Hermes. 2, 1. xviii, 15. March 12. Born in Rapho Township, Sept. 18, 1812. Wife of Timothy Grosh. Three of her four children survived her.

1020. **Matilda Louisa Enck.** 2, l. xviii, 14. March 14. Born in Warwick, Feb. 12, 1823; a daughter of John and Susan (Knauss) Seaber. Wife of Augustus Enck. She had eight children, of whom six survived her.

1021. **Karl Julius Mack.** 3, l. xv, 16. March 18. Born in Weissenburg, Germany, June 1, 1861.

1022. **Sarah Anna Conn.** 2, l. xviii, 13. March 31. Born in Emmaus, a daughter of Lewis Geitner, Nov. 25, 1797. Wife of Philip Conn.

1023. **Elizabeth Hostetter.** 2, l. xxiii, 19. April 12. Born Nov. 3, 1819; a daughter of Samuel Keller, of Lititz Mills. Wife of John S. Hostetter.

1024. **Francis William Christ.** 3, l. xx, 9. April 27. Born in Lititz, a son of Christian and Anna Julianna Christ (daughter of Peter Christ), Feb. 29, 1816. At the age of fifteen he was apprenticed to Jacob Greider with whom he served his time at shoemaking. In 1844 he married Sarah Ann Kraemer. Their three children died in early youth. Immediately after his marriage he and his wife assumed charge of the household department of John Beck's Academy; and there he devoted his time and energy to the material and spiritual welfare of the older boys of that institution. Deeply interested also in the young men of the congregation, he was appointed a deacon to have them under his especial care; and it is likely that this—amid much and varied usefulness to the community— was his greatest service. From 1855 until his death he was actively engaged in the Moravian Sunday School: first as its librarian, then as a teacher, and finally as the Assistant Superintendent. He served for many years as a member of the Board of Trustees; also, as the chief sacristan in the church. In public affairs a Justice of the Peace, he resigned his office, during President Grant's first administration, to accept that of Postmaster; and this trust he held to the close of his life.

1025. **William Andrew Schmidt.** 3, l. xx, 10. June 7. Born at Gross-Hepbach, Würtemberg, March 3, 1837. Came to America in 1852. Married Catharine Stark. By trade a stone-mason.

1026. **Sarah Ellen Buch.** 2, l. xvi, 1. June 20. Daughter of Elias and Maria (Grosh) Buch. Aged twenty-three years.

1027. **Howard Jacob Roth.** 3, l. v, 11. June 27. Child of Jacob Roth. Died of scarlet fever, aged nearly seven years.

1028. **Blanche Cordelia Keller.** 2, l. v, 9. July 18. Infant daughter of Thomas Keller.

1029. **Harry Regennas.** 3, l. v, 12. Aug. 21. Infant son of William Regennas.

1030. **Elmer Augustus Sturgis.** 3, l. v, 13. Sept. 3. Infant son of James O. Sturgis.

1031. **John Bender.** 3, l. xx, 11. Sept. 15. Born in Upper Leacock Township, Lancaster Co., May 7, 1825. Married Rebecca Bucer. Of fourteen children five survived him. A veterinary surgeon.

1032. **Emma Louisa Habecker.** 2, l. xv, 1. Oct. 5. Unmarried Sister. Born in Lititz, June 17, 1860; a daughter of Isaac and Rebecca (Reidenbach) Habecker.

1033. **John Reidenbach.** 3, l. xx, 1. Nov. 19. Born in Manheim Township, June 12, 1811; a son of Peter Reidenbach. Married Mary Burgess, who was his second wife, in 1855.

1034. **Albert Dieffenderfer.** 3, l. xv, 15. Nov. 19. Son of Samuel L. Dieffenderfer. Died of typhoid fever, aged seventeen years.

1035. **Samuel Adam Reidenbach.** 3, l. xv, 14. Nov. 19. A son of Adam B. Reidenbach. Died of typhoid fever, aged seventeen years.

1037. **John C. Ford.** 3, l. xx, 12. Dec. 12. Son of David Ford. Married Mary Lightner. By trade a stone-mason. Died of typhoid fever, aged twenty-seven years.

1884.

1038. **Louisa Catharine Kreiter.** 2, l. xiv, 15. Jan. 10. Daughter of Charles and Louisa Kreiter. Died of consumption, aged twenty-three years.

1039. **Samuel S. Bricker.** 3, l. xx, 13. Born April 10, 1807, in Shaeferstown, Pa. Married Elizabeth Fielis. Aged seventy-six years.

1040. **Anna Maria Keller.** 2, l. xviii, 12. March 15. Born in Lancaster, Sept. 23, 1798; a daughter of John and Catharine (Sheib) Kraemer. Wife of Frederick Keller. Died of pneumonia.

1041. **Ida Cecilia Hall.** 2, l. xiv, 14. April 29. Unmarried Sister. Born in Lititz, April 20, 1815; a daughter of Christian Hall. For forty years she was a teacher in Linden Hall Seminary.

1042. **Elizabeth Barr.** 2, l. xviii, 11. May 7. Born at Ephrata, Lancaster Co., Nov. 24, 1800. Widow of George M. Barr. Daughter of John and Catharine Holl.

1043. **Amelia Leah Muecke.** 2, l. xviii, 10. July 1. Born in Lititz, July 20, 1809; a daughter of Philip and Susanna (Albright) Bachman. In 1834 she married the widower Michael Muecke, with whom she had two children.

1044. **Leon Henry Milchsack.** 3, l. v, 14. Aug. 15. Infant son of Thomas Milchsack.

1045. **John Christian Keller.** 3, l. xx, 14. Sept. 24. Son of Samuel Keller, of Lititz Mills. Aged fifty-two years.

1046. **Matthias Tshudy Huebener.** 3, l. xx, 15. Oct. 8. Born in Friedland, N. C., Jan. 1, 1826; a son of the Rev. Samuel and Salome (Tshudy) Huebener. He received his fine education in the Lititz Academy, in Nazareth Hall, and in the Moravian Theological Seminary. After some years of employment as a clerk in the stores of Senseman, in Nazareth, and Pfohl, in Salem, N. C., he came to Lititz and here accepted a like position with his uncle, Jacob Tshudy; afterwards entering into partnership with him, and later with his son. When the Lititz Deposit Bank was organized he became its cashier; and with the establishment of the Lititz National Bank he received the same appointment, keeping it until his death. In 1873 he was married to Mary S. Lichtenthaeler. They had three

children—one daughter and two sons; both of whom—the Revs.
Louis and Robert Huebener—are now serving the Church. As a
musician, he was a member of the Lititz Philharmonic Society, and
in the church-music he played the flute and bass-trombone. Died
suddenly, of heart disease, while attending to the furnace in the
basement of the bank.

1047. **Thomas Sands.** 3, l. xix, 1. Oct. 9. His wife's maiden name was
Stuber. Aged eighty-eight years.

1048. **James Henry Miksch.** 3, l. xx, 16. Nov. 18. Born near Nazareth,
Feb. 5, 1818; a son of Nathaniel and Julianna Miksch. Established
a tinsmith shop in Lititz in 1840. In 1841 he married Cecilia Louisa
Brunner, of Nazareth, who died in 1844. His second marriage, 1845,
was to Matilda Kreider. He served the community as a school-
director, and the congregation as a trustee and an elder; and was
for years one of the sacristans (*dieners*) of the church. Of his
seven children, five survived their father.

1049. **Charles Rudolph Kreiter.** 3, l. xix, 2. Dec. 28. Born in Lititz,
March 10, 1812; a son of Benjamin and Anna Maria Kreiter. Married Elizabeth Bandon. Not a Moravian in later life.

1885.

1050. **Anna Elizabeth Miller.** 2, l. xviii, 9. Feb. 7. The widow of Jacob
Miller, farmer, who resided near Lititz. Her maiden name was
Hoover. Aged ninety-eight years.

1051. **Charles Addison Lichtenthaeler.** 3, l. xix, 3. Born in Lititz, April
13, 1836; a son of Samuel Lichtenthaeler. Served in the Civil War
—Pennsylvania cavalry. Spent the last seven years of his life in
Reading. Aged forty-eight years.

1052. **Wesley Morton Sturgis.** 3, l. v, 15. Nov. 7, 1891. Son of Nathan
O. Sturgis. Diphtheria. Aged nearly three years.

1053. **Mary Elizabeth Gochenauer.** 2, l. v, 8. June 10. Daughter of
Albert Gochenauer. Infant.

1054. **Helen Kauffman.** 2, l. v, 7. July 5. Infant daughter of Jacob
Kauffman.

1055. **Laura Eliza Lutz.** 2, l. v, 6. Infant daughter of Benjamin Lutz.

1056. **Howard Regennas.** 3, l. v, 16. Infant son of William Regennas.

1057. **Albertus E. Stark.** 3, l. iv, 1. Sept. 22. Infant son of Samuel
Stark.

1058. **Lillian Mary Erlington Oehme.** 2, l. v, 5. Nov. 13. Infant
daughter of Henry Oehme.

1059. **Emma Holtzhouse.** 2, l. xviii, 18. Nov. 18. A daughter of Benjamin Badorf. Wife of Hiram Holtzhouse. Died of typhoid fever,
aged twenty-six years.

1060. **Allan Hamilton.** 3, l. xix, 4. Dec. 22. He was born in Glasgow,
Scotland, March 27, 1814. In his early manhood he removed to
England, whence, in 1837, at the instance of Sir Fowell Buxton, he
went to St. Lucia, W. I., as a teacher to the freedmen. Here he en-
dured great trials; was assaulted and violently beaten by a planter,
and came near dying of yellow fever. Later he founded a training

school for native teachers in Antigua, and there he became acquainted with the Brethren. In 1844 he was ordained, by Bishop Martin of England, as a Deacon of the Church. Then, as a Moravian missionary, he served successively in St. Croix, Antigua, St. Thomas (there also filling the office of Government Inspector of Schools) and Jamaica. In 1865 he married the widow Ely, m.n. Moore. Retired from service in 1870, and in 1871 came to Lititz. There, as far as his health permitted, he was active in the Sunday School,and as a home-missionary in the adjacent country, preaching frequently in the old Moravian Church at Donegal. In 1879 he returned to England, where, his health having been temporarily restored, he labored earnestly in several of our congregations, especially at Bristol. In October, 1885, he returned to America, hoping to spend his last days in Salem, N. C.; but illness was upon him before he reached the South, and he died soon after his arrival in Salem. The Rt. Rev. J. Taylor Hamilton is one of his sons by a former wife.

1061. **Ann Eliza Rickert.** 2, l. xviii, 7. Dec. 28. Born May 17, 1840; a daughter of David Becker. Wife of Charles Rickert.

1886.

1062. **Ruth Naomi Beck.** 2, l. v, 4. Jan. 14. Daughter of John and Anne Beck. Aged three years.

1063. **Haydn Hull Tshudy.** 3, l. iv, 2. Jan. 24. A son of Haydn H. Tshudy. Aged five years.

1064. **Barbara Eliza Regennas.** 2, l. xiv, 13. Feb. 24. Unmarried Sister, of the Lancaster congregation. Born Jan. 31, 1819; a daughter of John Jacob Regennas.

1065. **Charles Stark.** 3, l. iv, 3. May 6. Son of Martin Stark. Aged ten years.

1066. **Harry Carpenter Hull.** 3, l. xix, 5. May 21. A son of Dr. Levi Hull. Aged nearly thirty-five years. His widow, a granddaughter of General John A. Sutter, and two sons survived him.

1067. **Maggie May Meily.** 2, l. v, 3. June 2. Daughter of Linnaeus Meily. Died of diphtheria, aged six years.

1068. **Minnie Minerva Meily.** 2, l. v, 2. June 6. Sister of the foregoing. Diphtheria.

1069. **Beatus Kreiter.** 3, l. iv, 4. July 6. ⎫
1070. **Beatus Kreiter.** 3, l. iv, 4. July 6. ⎬ Twin sons of Ralph Kreiter.

1071. **Beata Becker.** 2, l. v, 1.

1072. **Elizabeth Miller.** 2, l. xiv, 12. Aug 29. Unmarried Sister. Daughter of Jacob Miller. Aged sixty-three years.

1073. **Sarah Caroline Christ.** 2, l. iv, 16. Sept. 27. Infant daughter of Albert Christ.

1074. **Albert Lutz.** 3, l. iv, 5. Sept. 28. Infant son of Benjamin Lutz.

1075. **Salome Kreiter.** 2, l. xiv, 11. Oct. 22. Unmarried Sister. Daughter of Michael Christian Kreiter and his wife Regina, m.n. Buehler. Aged eighty-four years.

1076. **Susanna Grosh.** 2, l. xviii, 6. Oct. 31. Born at Pine Hill, near Lititz, April 21, 1807. Her maiden name was Shober. Wife of Charles A. Grosh.

1077. **John Souder.** 3, l. xix, 6. Born at Kissel Hill, near Lititz, April 24, 1832. Married Ellen Muecke. Aged fifty-four years. A blacksmith.

1078. **Anna Greider.** 2, l. xvii, 16. Dec. 31. Wife of John F. Greider. Aged sixty-seven years.

1887.

1079. **Beatus Miksch.** 3, l. iv, 6. March 14. Son of Haydn N. Miksch.

1080. **Joseph Oliver Sturgis.** 3, l. iv, 7. Infant son of Edwin Sturgis.

1081. **Beatus Bender.** 3, l. xiv, 8. May 27. ⎫
1082. **Beatus Bender.** 3, l. xiv, 8. May 27. ⎬ Twin sons of W. K. Bender.

1083. **Beata Harry.** 2, l. iv, 15. July 7. Daughter of John Harry.

1084. **Horace Roy Roth.** 3, l. iv, 9. Aug. 28. Infant son of Horace Roth.

1085. **Elmer James Sturgis.** 3, l. iv, 10. Aug. 31. Infant son of Horace Sturgis.

1086. **Isaac Holl.** 3, l. xix, 7. Sept. 5. Born in Ephrata Township, Jan. 11, 1803; a son of John and Catharine (Beck) Holl. In 1826 he married Margaret Waechter; four sons, one daughter. His second marriage was to Mary Ann Whitecraft; five sons, two daughters.

1087. **Susan Enck.** 2, l. xvii, 15. Oct. 8. Wife of B. Franklin Enck. Her maiden name was Buchter. Aged forty-two years.

1088. **Beatus Beck.** 3, l. iv, 11. ⎫
1089. **Beatus Beck.** 3, l. iv, 11. ⎬ Twin sons of John and Annie Beck.

1090. **Isaac Habecker.** 3, l. xix, 8. Nov. 19. Born in Lincoln, Lancaster Co., Jan. 23, 1836; a son of Adam Habecker. Married Rebecca Reidenbach. Had five children. A house-painter.

1091. **Susan Huber,** m.n. Weidler. 2, l. xvii, 14. Dec. 16. Born Oct. 23, 1833. Wife of John Huber. Ten children survived her.

1092. **Matilda Diehm.** 2, l. xvii, 13. Dec. 20. Daughter of Samuel Stoever, and widow of Philip Diehm. Born March 6, 1817.

1888.

1093. **James Alexander Sturgis.** 3, l. xix, 9. Feb. 26. Born in Lititz, Jan. 3, 1814; a son of Samuel Sturgis. His first marriage was to Verona Huber; his second to Sarah Rudy. Two sons and two daughters of the former survived him. He served the church in various capacities. Followed the trade of carpentry.

1094. **Elizabeth Kreiter,** m.n. Bandon. 2, l. xvii, 12. Feb. 26. Born March 5, 1812. Wife of Charles R. Kreiter.

1095. **Anna M. Haughman.** 2, l. iv, 14. Aug. 2. Infant daughter of D. M. Haughman.

1096. **Paulina Lavina Frederick.** 2, l. xiv, 10. Sept. 12. Unmarried Sister. Daughter of Christian Frederick. Aged sixty-five years.

1097. **Elizabeth Kreiter.** 2, l. xvii, 11. Nov. 23. Born in York, Pa., March 12, 1797; a daughter of Jacob Westhaeffer. Was one of the first day-pupils of Linden Hall Seminary. Married Samuel Kreiter.

Two sons, three daughters, twenty-nine grand and thirty-nine great-grandchildren. Served the church in various ways. Aged nearly ninety-two years.

1098. **David H. Brunner.** 3, l. xix, 10. Nov. 25. Born at Reinholdsville, Lancaster Co., Aug. 15, 1825. With his brother he carried on the foundry business at Brunnerville, near Lititz, for twenty-eight years. Married Frances H. Longenecker. Died of an apoplectic stroke.

1099. **Mary Kreider.** 2, l. xiv, 9. Dec. 30. Unmarried Sister. Daughter of Charles Kreider. Aged nearly twenty-five years.

1889.

1100. **Beatus Haines.** 3, l. iv, 12. Jan. 5. Son of Frederick C. Haines.

1101. **Edward Samuel Sturgis.** 3, l. xix, 11. Feb. 4. Born in Lititz, Nov. 13, 1828; a son of Samuel and Susan (Correll) Sturgis. Married Rosanna L. Oehme. Of eight children, six survived him. He was the first owner and landlord of the Sturgis House. Served in the Civil War—Nevin's Independent Battery I.

1101b. **Walter Correll Keller.** 3, l. iii, 2. Aug. 28 (1891). Infant son of Thomas Keller.

1102. **Marie Eschbach,** m.n. Leclaire. 2, l. xvii, 10. Feb. 25. Born in Vergaville, France. Came to this country with her husband, Joseph Eschbach, in 1856, and united with the Moravian Church in 1872. Her genial, happy disposition and kind heart won her many friends. Died of pneumonia, aged seventy years.

1102b. **John F. Harry.** 3, l. xix, 12. May 31 (1890). Born in E. Hempfield Township, June 4, 1859. Married Lavinia F. Lutz. Bitten by a strange dog that was not supposed to be rabid, he was seized, three months later, by a violent attack of hydrophobia which caused his death.

1102c. **Robert Martin Bowman.** 3, l. iii, 1. June 2 (1891). Son of Jacob and Arabella Bowman. Died of diphtheria, aged nine years.

1103. **Beata Bender.** 2, l. iv, 13. Aug. 22. Child of W. K. Bender.

1890.

1103b. **Walter Birney Oehme.** 3, l. iv, 16. June 17 (1891). Infant son of Birney Oehme.

1104. **Frances H. Brunner,** m.n. Longenecker. 2, l. xvii, 9. March 4. Born Sept. 12, 1826. Wife of David H. Brunner.

1104b. **Francis Christ Bowman.** 3, l. iv, 15. June 3 (1891). Son of Jacob Bowman. Diphtheria. Eight years.

1105. **Annie S. Kummer.** 2, l. xvii, 8. Oct. 30. Born in E. Hempfield Township, April 22, 1834. Wife of the Rev. Joseph H. Kummer. Served, with her husband, the Moravian First Churches of New York and Philadelphia.

1105b. **Harry Palm.** 3, l. iv, 14. June 3 (1891). Infant son of Albert Palm.

1106. **William Edward Buck.** 3, l. iv, 13. Aug. 3. Infant son of Joseph H. Buck.

7

1107. **George Edward Keller.** 3, l. xix, 13. Dec. 26. Born in Lititz, Sept. 15, 1822; a son of Frederick H. Keller. For many years he served the congregation; first as one of its sacristans, and then as its sexton. On Second Christmas Day, while walking towards his home, he was stricken with sudden death.

1891.

1108. **Mary M. Miley.** 2, l. iv, 12. Jan. 10. Daughter of Linnaeus Miley. Died of diphtheria, aged five years.

1108b. **Augustus Enck.** 3, l. xix, 14. Aug. 8. Born in Lexington, near Lititz, Nov. 11, 1816. Married Matilda Seaber. After an apoplectic stroke his end was hastened by an attack of pneumonia. By trade a house-carpenter.

N. B.—For
  Robert M. Bowman, see 1102c.
  Walter B. Oehme, see 1103b.
  Francis Christ Bowman, see 1104b.
  Lizzie Selina Yerger, see 1110.
  Harry Palm, see 1105b.
  Walter C. Keller, see 1101b.

1109. **Lillian May Furlow.** 2, l. iv, 11. July 10. Daughter of Andrew Furlow. Aged five years.

1109b. **Susan Shultz Brickenstein.** 2, l. xvii, 7. Aug. 28. Born in Friedberg, N. C., Aug. 1, 1836; a daughter of Bishop Henry A. Shultz. With her husband, the Rev. Hermann A. Brickenstein, she served in the congregations of Olney, Ill., and Brooklyn, N. Y., and for eighteen years she was the mistress of Linden Hall Seminary, a responsible position for which she was eminently qualified. Herself a fine soprano singer, she was a superior teacher of vocal music, and her masterful advice in regard to the training of the institution's chorus was always gladly accepted and applied by its instructor. In loving remembrance of her, the teachers and pupils of 1873-1892 erected a memorial window in the chapel of the school.

1892.

1109c. **George Heiserman.** 3, l. xix, 15. Jan. 16. Born in Germany (Oberamt Marbach), Nov. 3, 1829. Emigrated to America in 1852. Married Catharine Kling. Two sons survived him. Served in the Civil War—Nevin's Independent Battery I.

1110. **Lizzie Selina Yerger.** 2, l. iv, 10. Nov. 11 (1891). Daughter of John Yerger. Died of diphtheria, aged eleven years.

1111. **Catharine Kling,** m.n. Schauffer. 2, l. xvii, 6. Jan. 31. Born in Lancaster Co., April 29, 1864. Wife of Amos Kling.

1112. **Christiana Kreider.** 2, l. xvii, 5. Feb. 27. Born Dec. 12, 1830. Her maiden name was Stormfeltz. Wife of Martin Kreider.

1113. **Harry Kling.** 3, l. xv, 13. March 14. Son of Frederick and Catharine Kling. Died of consumption, aged twenty-three years.

1114. **Juliana Shoenlein.** 2, l. xiv, 8. May 12. She was a daughter of John and Elizabeth (Ricksecker) Shoenlein. Born in Lititz, May 12, 1809. Served the congregation faithfully in various capacities.

1115. **Beatus Sturgis.** 3, l. iii, 3. Aug. 18. Child of Edwin Sturgis.

1116. **Henry Harrison Grosh.** 3, l. xix, 16. Oct. 15. Born in Lititz, Feb. 4, 1837; a son of Charles A. Grosh. Married Caroline Oehme. Of eight children, four sons and two daughters survived him. By trade a carriage-maker. Served in the Civil War—Nevin's Independent Battery I.

1893.

1116b. **Arthur Harrison Becker.** 3, l. iii, 4. Infant son of Scott Becker.

1117. **Laura Isabelle Tshudy.** 2, l. xiv, 7. May 5. Born in Lititz, Oct. 2, 1878. Daughter of Haydn H. and Emma J. (Hull) Tshudy.

1118. **Frederick Charles Haines.** 3, l. xviii, 1. June 1. Born at Red Lion, York Co., Jan. 7, 1866. Married Mary E. Heiser. At the time of his death he was serving his second term as constable of the borough. Typhoid fever.

1119. **William Washington Oehme.** 3, l. xviii, 2. June 14. Born in Brunnerville, near Lititz, Feb. 12, 1825; a son of Christian and Margaret (Gernand) Oehme. Married Barbara Conrad. Served his country faithfully for four years in the Civil War—Co. D, 99th Penna. Volunteers.

1120. **Maria Anna Schmidt.** 2, l. xvii, 4. Aug. 19. Daughter of John Bucher, and wife of Emmanuel Schmidt. Died in Lancaster, aged fifty-eight years.

1121. **Sarah M. Bomberger.** 2, l. xvii, 3. Sept. 1. Born in Manor Township, a daughter of Jacob Brenneman, Dec. 26, 1858. Wife of Isaac F. Bomberger. Three daughters survived her.

1122. **Catharine Lichtenthaeler.** 2, l. xvii, 2. Dec. 9. Born in Lancaster, a daughter of John Kraemer, June 23, 1808. In 1830 she was married to Samuel Lichtenthaeler. Two daughters and one son survived her. Her death resulted from a second stroke of apoplexy.

1123. **Adam Hambright.** 3, l. xviii, 3. Dec. 14. Born in Eden, Manheim Township, Oct. 18, 1817. Was married first to Elizabeth Brunner, and secondly to Caroline Zitzman.

1124. **Jacob Harrison Graver.** 3, l. xviii, 4. Dec. 17. Born at Rothsville, Lancaster Co., May 12, 1855; a son of Jacob Graver. Married Emeline Hollinger.

1894.

1125. **Rachel Maria Nievling.** 2, l. xvii, 1. Feb. 23. Born April 18, 1810; a daughter of Peter Abraham Kreiter. Married first to William Kraemer, and secondly to Jacob Nievling.

1126. **Ferdinand Daniel Rickert.** 3, l. xviii, 5. March 25. Born in Warwick, Feb. 21, 1820; a son of Daniel Rickert. After the death of his mother, when he was about four years old, he was adopted by Christian and Magdalena Miksch, and when they accepted a call to the Indian Mission, in Canada, he was transferred to the care of Henry Blickensderfer with whom he learned cigar-making until he was apprenticed to Charles H. Kryder, of Warwick, to learn tailoring. Having employed his leisure time in study under the instruction of his brother John, his services as a teacher were secured for the Lititz Academy, in which institution he taught the higher classes from 1840 to 1865, when, upon John Beck's relinquishment of the school, he became one of its principals, in partnership with George W. Hepp, continuing as such until 1881. His first marriage was to Emma E. Wolle, a daughter of the Rev. Peter Wolle, who died in 1866; his second marriage was to Elvira C. Dysart. Although of a diffident manner and retiring disposition, he was a man of refined artistic tastes, standing high in his profession and valued in the community. He had also considerable experience as a scrivener and a surveyor, and as an architect he was the designer of the Lititz Moravian Chapel. Some of the best tombstone work on our graveyard was sculptured by him. Two daughters, of his first marriage, survived him.

1127. **Julia Ann Derr.** 2, l. xxiv, 1. April 2. Born near Washingtonville, Montour County, Sept. 28, 1821; a daughter of James Madden. Wife of Dr. J. W. Derr. Of five children, two sons and one daughter survived her.

1128. **Susan Beam.** 2, l. xxiv, 2. May 17. Born at York, July 6, 1805; a daughter of Samuel Sturgis. Married Samuel Beam. One son and two daughters survived her.

1129. **Sarah Ann Christ.** 2, l. xxiv, 3. June 23. Born in Lancaster, Jan. 6, 1816; a daughter of John and Catharine (Scheib) Kraemer. Widow of Francis W. Christ.

1130. **Samuel Frederick Van Vleck.** 3, l. xviii, 6. Sept. 21. Born in Nazareth, Oct. 14, 1855; a son of Bishop Henry Jacob Van Vleck and his wife Augusta Sophia, m.n. Beear. After living with his parents in South Bethlehem and in Gnadenhütten, Ohio, he came, in 1876, to Lititz, and was engaged by the Moravian congregation as its organist and choirmaster. In 1881 he was married to Elizabeth Miller, an adopted daughter of Abraham Van Vleck. Desirous of making himself more proficient in music, he went with that purpose in view in September, 1893, to Leipzig; but there his health, which had never been robust, began to fail, and he was compelled, after some months' absence, to return to his home, which he reached only to die soon afterwards. For many years he was Treasurer of the congregation, and he served the Church faithfully in other ways.

1131. **Ella Gertrude Gochenaur.** 2, l. iv, 9. Nov. 11. Infant daughter of Albert Gochenaur. Died of whooping-cough and pneumonia.

1132. **Barbara Oehme,** m.n. Conrad. 2, l. xxiv, 4. Dec. 22. Born Sept. 2, 1826. Widow of William W. Oehme. Had been afflicted for many years with epilepsy. Her end came suddenly as she was crossing from the home of one of her children to that of another.

1895.

1133. **Ralph Smith.** 3, l. iii, 5. Jan. 1. Infant son of William and Anna C. Smith.

1134. **Henry Linnaeus Oehme.** 3, l. xviii, 7. Jan. 17. Son of William W. Oehme. Married Hannah E. M. Sherzer. By trade a house-painter; but latterly he carried on a local barber's shop. Aged forty-two years.

1135. **Emma Jane Tshudy.** 2, l. xxiv, 5. Jan. 27. Born in Warwick, Nov. 17, 1843; a daughter of Dr. Levi Hull. She was educated in Linden Hall Seminary, later became a teacher there, and subsequently for a number of years filled the position of teacher of music in the Public Schools of Lebanon, Pa. In 1868 she was married to Haydn H. Tshudy. Her husband, two daughters, and one son survived her.

1136. **Paulina Elizabeth Tshudy.** 2, l. xiv, 6. March 12. Unmarried Sister. Born in Lititz, Jan. 16, 1813; youngest daughter of Matthias Tshudy. Educated in Linden Hall Seminary. Possessed of a fine alto voice, she was a valuable member of the church-choir. Served for twenty-five years as a Sunday-school teacher, and was actively interested, likewise, in the Women's Missionary and other societies of the church. In May, 1893, she fell in her room, fracturing her hip; and from this injury she never recovered.

1137. **Beata Heiserman.** 2, l. iv, 8. July 4. Child of John J. Heiserman.

1138. **Agnes Amelia Grosh.** 2, l. xiv, 5. July 21. Unmarried Sister. Born in Lititz, July 28, 1846. A daughter of Charles A. Grosh. After her mother's death she removed to Bethlehem, making her home with her sister, Mrs. Lawall; and there, of a cancer, she died.

1139. **Blanche Irene Sturgis.** 2, l. iv, 7. Nov. 17. Born Nov. 19, 1889. Child of Edgar Sturgis.

1140. **Margaret Ann Dysart.** 2, l. xiv, 4. Dec. 4. Born in Mount Joy, Lancaster Co., July 10, 1831. Unmarried Sister.

1896.

1141. **Sarah M. Beam.** 2, l. xxiv, 6. March 17. Born in Lititz, Jan. 25, 1822; a daughter of Samuel Sturgis. Married Abraham Beam. She lived, successively, in Lancaster and Lebanon, and removed to Lititz in 1895.

1142. **Sabina Amelia Muecke.** 2, l. xiv, 3. April 4. Unmarried Sister. Born in Lititz, May 8, 1821; a daughter of Michael and Lydia Muecke. She was the last resident Sister in the Sisters' House. An attack of apoplexy caused her death.

1143. **Maria Bicking.** 2, l. xxiv, 7. Aug. 3. Born in Warwick, Nov. 6, 1824; a daughter of John Seaber. Married to James Bicking. In 1868 she removed with her family to Philadelphia, where she resided about ten years, when they returned to Lititz. Suffered in her final year from a disease of a cancerous nature.

1144. **Naomi Longenecker.** 2, l. iv, 6. Sept. 23. Infant daughter of William Longenecker.

1897.

1145. **Rosanna Louisa Sturgis.** 2, l. xxiv, 8. Jan. 3. Born in Lexington, Lancaster Co., Oct. 28, 1831; a daughter of Christian Oehme. In 1849 she was married to Edward S. Sturgis. They had eight children; two sons died in their infancy.

1146. **Henry Schoenberger.** 3, l. xviii, 8. Jan. 3. Born in York Co., Feb. 21, 1824. Was twice married; first to Eliza Martzall, and secondly to Catharine Ressler.

1147. **Nancy Niess.** 2, l. xiv, 2. April 12. Unmarried. Aged seventy-seven years.

1148. **Joseph Horsfield Kummer.** 3, l. xviii, 9. April 23. Born in Bethlehem, June 28, 1820. After spending many years as a missionary in the West Indies, he became the pastor of the congregations in New York, Lancaster, and Philadelphia. For a number of years he was a minister in the Presbyterian Church. After his return to the Moravian Church, he served the congregation in Coopersburg for about a year. Was twice married; first to Amelia C. Reichel, and secondly to Annie S. Meyers. Spent the last years of his life in Lancaster. He was an eloquent preacher.

1149. **Charles Franklin Buch.** 3, l. iii, 6. July 27. Infant son of J. Franklin Buch.

1150. **Paul Lewis Buck.** 3, l. iii, 7. Aug. 29. Infant son of Joseph Buck.

1151. **Sophia Magdalena Regennas.** 2, l. xxiv, 9. Sept. 26. Born in Warwick, Oct. 25, 1823; a daughter of John Miller. Married William Henry Regennas. She served the community as a sick-nurse, and in preparing the dead for burial. She had two daughters and three sons.

1152. **Beata Oehme.** 2, l. iv, 5. Oct. 1. Child of Birney Oehme.

1153. **Annie C. Smith.** 2, l. xxiv, 10. Nov. 19. Daughter of John Carpenter. Wife of William Smith. Died of consumption, aged twenty-five years.

1898.

1154. **Edith Caroline Huber.** 2, l. iv, 4. Jan. 22. Infant daughter of S. M. Huber.

1155. **Charles Augustus Grosh.** 3, l. xv, 12. March 10. Unmarried. Born in Lititz, Dec. 1, 1866. A son of H. Harrison Grosh. Was one of the ushers in the church. Not a bright young man; but such a good, helpful fellow, and so popular, that his many friends, at his funeral, completely filled the church.

1156. **George Theodore Greider.** 3, l. xviii, 10. April 14. Born in Lititz, March 10, 1815; a son of Jacob and Juliana (Christ) Greider. In 1845 he married Emma Bear, of Lancaster. For many years he engaged in the shoe business and for a time was the landlord of the Lititz Springs Hotel. Because of his excellent memory, he was, in his old age, a link between the far past and the present, and being ever willing to impart his recollections, he was often called upon for antiquarian information. He had one child, a daughter, who married Dr. O. T. Huebener, of Lancaster.

1157. **Karl Schick.** 3, l. xviii, 11. May 21. Born in Urbach, Würtemberg, March 29, 1836. Emigrated to America and came to Lititz in 1893. Married Philippine Weissert. A carpet-weaver.

1158. **Beatus Huber.** 3, l. iii, 8. Child of John L. Huber.

1159. **Elizabeth Stark.** 2, l. xxiv, 11. July 31. Wife of Charles Stark. Aged eighty-seven years.

1899.

1160. **Benjamin Gingrich.** 3, l. xv, 11. Jan. 9. Unmarried. Born April 4, 1818; a son of Jacob and Elizabeth (Bomberger) Gingrich. In 1844 he was engaged as the farmer of the Linden Hall Seminary land, and he continued in that work until the farm was abandoned in 1888, when he was employed in other duties about the school. He served under Principals Frueauff, Bechler, Reichel and Brickenstein. Was also a *diener* in the church.

1161. **Jacob Weitzel.** 3, l. xviii, 12. March 27. Born in Ingelheim, near Mainz, June 28, 1815. Came to this country in 1839, and in 1840 to Lititz. Here he rented and afterwards purchased the old Lititz brewery, continuing in that business for nineteen years. In 1841 he was married to Lisetta Hamm. They had one child—a daughter. In 1859 he sold his brewery and removed to Green Bay, Wisconsin, where he built and operated a vinegar factory. Returned to Lititz in 1863. A genial, gifted man, with considerable poetic talent; hospitable and kind; always ready with his helping hand for the needy.

1162. **Nathaniel Shober Wolle.** 3, l. xviii, 13. Feb. 11. He was born in Bethania, N. C., Oct. 9, 1822; a son of Bishop Peter Wolle and Maria Theresa, m.n. Shober. Educated in Nazareth Hall and in the Moravian Theological Seminary. In 1845 he came to Lititz, bought out the Congregation store, and continued in that business until 1881, when he accepted a clerkship in the Lititz National Bank, later becoming its cashier. He married Angelica L. Miksch, of Nazareth. On June 29, 1896, they celebrated their Golden Wedding. He organized the Lititz Moravian Sunday School, and served it faithfully for fifty years, much of that time as its Superintendent. In the Church he filled various offices, having been a member of the Board of Trustees for twenty-five years, an Elder, a Deacon, and, at the time of his death, the Treasurer of the Congregation. In his time he sang as a bass in the Church Choir, and served also as a trombonist. Two sons and a daughter survived him.

1163. **Florence Theresa Rickert.** 2, l. xiv, 1. April 13. Unmarried Sister. Born in Lititz, April 7, 1848; a daughter of Ferdinand and Emma (Wolle) Rickert. She was a Deaconess of the congregation.

1164. **Josephine J. Delbo,** m.n. Sturgis. 2, l. xxiv, 12. Died in Lancaster and buried here May 8. Wife of Darius Delbo.

1165. **Elwood E. Stark.** 3, l. xv, 10. June 6. A son of Samuel and Mary (Enck) Stark. Died of consumption, aged sixteen years.

1166. **Willie Miller.** 3, l. iii, 9. Sept. 21. Child of George Miller. Died of diphtheria, aged eight years.

1167. **Maria Bender.** 2, l. xiii, 1. Oct. 6. Unmarried Sister. Daughter of John and Elizabeth Bender. Aged eighty-three years.

1169. **Charles Richard Miksch.** 3, l. xv, 8. Oct. 11. Born in Lititz, Dec. 2, 1881; a son of Alonzo and Lillian (Backius) Miksch.

1171. **Christian Storz.** 3, l. xviii, 14. Oct. 25. Born in Stoetzlingen, Würtemberg, June 19, 1832. Became a member of the Brethren's Church in Königsfeld. Came to America, 1863.

1172. **Sarah Cornelia Gingrich.** 2, l. xiii, 2. Oct. 28. Unmarried Sister. Daughter of Jacob Gingrich. Born in Rome, near Lititz, Nov. 6, 1828. She spent many years in the employ of Linden Hall Seminary, and for a long time had charge of the old Moravian Chapel.

1173. **Ann Frederick.** 2, l. xxiv, 13. Nov. 9. Born Nov. 3, 1826. Many years of her life were spent in the service of Linden Hall.

1174. **Margaret Janet Downey.** 2, l. xxiv, 14. Nov. 11. Born in Lancaster, Sept. 13, 1833; a daughter of Barnes E. Broom.

1175. **Nathan C. Fry.** 3, l. xviii, 15. Nov. 21. Born in Millport, Lancaster Co., Oct. 15, 1851. Married Anna Miksch. Served the Church faithfully for eighteen years as a Trustee, was the Assistant Superintendent of the Sunday School, and also a member of the church-choir. A highly esteemed man.

1900.

1176. **Mary Catharine Stark.** 2, l. xxiv, 15. Jan. 7. Born in Warwick, Sept. 22, 1846. She was the oldest daughter of Augustus and Matilda Enck. Wife of Samuel Stark.

1177. **Maria Buch.** 2, l. xxiv, 16. March 11. Born in Lititz, July 9, 1827; a daughter of Charles A. and Susan Grosh. Married Elias Buch. Of five children, one daughter survived her.

1178. **Caroline Zentmyer.** 2, l. xxv, 1. April 19. Born in Warwick, Dec. 17, 1830. A daughter of Thomas Sands; widow of B. G. Zentmyer.

1179. **Beata Weltmer.** 2, l. iv, 3. Aug. 29. Child of Paul Weltmer.

1180. **Marion Longenecker.** 2, l. iv, 2. Oct. 4. Infant of W. Longenecker.

1181. **David Marcus Bowman.** 3, l. xv, 7. Oct. 5. Son of Jacob Bowman. Died of typhoid fever, aged fourteen years.

1182. **Miriam Longenecker.** 2, l. iv, 1. Oct. 10. Twin sister of the foregoing M. L.

1183. **Charles William Grosh.** 3, l. iii, 11. Oct. 11. Infant of C. William and May (Siegfried) Grosh.

1185. **Mary Ann Enck.** 2, l. xxv, 2. Nov. 12. Born March 10, 1824. Widow on Andrew Enck. Her maiden name was Brunner.

1186. **Kathleen Olive Pfautz.** 2, l. iii, 16. Nov. 12. Child of Otis Pfautz.

1901.

1187. **William Henry Regennas.** 3, l. xvii, 1. Jan. 16. Born in Lititz, Oct. 30, 1820; a son of John Jacob Regennas. Married Sophia M. Miller. They celebrated their Golden Wedding in 1897. Three sons and one daughter survived him.

1188. **Aaron M. Diehm.** 3, l. iii, 12. Infant of William and Ada Diehm.

1189. **Juliet Rickert Harbison,** m.n. Rock. 2, l. xxv, 3. May 20. Born Sept. 14, 1814. Her first husband was John Rickert.

1190. **Violet Bender.** 2, l. iii, 15. July 2. Infant of John T. and Annie Bender.

1191. **Magdalene Bender.** 2, l. iii, 14. Dec. 3. Twin sister of the foregoing.

1192. **William Mohn Carper.** 3, l. xvii, 2. Dec. 3. A son of Samuel Carper. Died of consumption, aged twenty-nine years.

1902.

1193. **John Huber.** 3, l. xvii, 3. March 31. A son of Abraham and Maria (Bear) Huber, he was born July 2, 1822, on the old homestead about one mile north of Lititz, and always lived on a part of the original farm bought from the Penns by his ancestors. In 1851 he was married to Susan Weidler. They had four sons and seven daughters. Two of the latter, Mary and Emma, wife of the Rev. Samuel Rock, have served as Moravian missionaries in Alaska. An expert farmer and fruit-grower.

1194. **Emma Elizabeth Haisch.** 2, l. xxv, 4. April 6. Born in Rome, near Lititz, June 13, 1845; a daughter of William and Eliza Diehm. Wife of Christian F. Haisch. Five of seven children survived her.

1195. **Erna Naomi Sturgis.** 2, l. xiii, 14. April 28. Daughter of Edwin Sturgis. Died of typhoid fever, aged thirteen years.

1196. **Jacob Palm.** 3, l. xviii, 16. May 14. Born near Schoeneck, Lancaster Co., Jan. 8, 1837. Married Louisa Diehm. Served his country in the Civil War,—79th Regt. Penna. Volunteers.

1197. **Catharine Elizabeth Conrad.** 2, l. xxi, 6. July 11. Born April 22, 1827. Widow of George Conrad. Her maiden name was Oehme.

1198. **Mildred E. Longenecker.** 2, l. iii, 13. Sept. 2. Child of Wayne Longenecker.

1199. **Caroline Sophia Baker.** 2, l. xxv, 5. Sept. 8. Born in Lititz, Jan. 26, 1822; a daughter of Samuel and Susanna Sturgis, and a twin sister of Sarah M. Beam. In 1845 she was married to C. Edwin Ricksecker, who died in 1848. Their son is J. Tyler Ricksecker. Her second marriage was to Joseph Baker.

1200. **James M. Bicking** 3, l. xvii, 4. Nov. 4. Born in Philadelphia, March 20, 1820. He married Maria E. Seaber. As the owner and driver of the daily stage between Lititz and Lancaster, for many years, he was well known to a large number of people.

1201. **Charles Henry Seaber.** 3, l. xvii, 5. Nov. 29. Born in Warwick, July 26, 1828; a son of John Jacob and Susanna (Knauss) Seaber. Married Mary Catharine Weidler. Of eight children, four sons survived him. By occupation a farmer.

1202. **Rebecca Louisa Habecker.** 2, l. xxv, 6. Dec. 10. Born in Manheim Township, June 16, 1838; a daughter of Jacob and Rebecca Reidenbach. In 1859 she was married to Isaac S. Habecker.

1203. **Samuel Emmanuel Grosh.** 3, l. xvii, 6. Dec. 30. He was born in Lititz, Oct. 10, 1834; a son of Charles A. and Susan (Shober) Grosh. After he had received his education in John Beck's Litiz Academy, he learned the blackmith's trade of his father and then worked at the same for some time in Allentown. Returned to Lititz, he entered into partnership with his brother, Harrison, (1857) in the carriage-making business, his own department being the smithy. In 1858 he married Amanda C. Kraemer. He served the community efficiently on the School Board and in the Borough Council, and was for twelve years a Trustee and for more than twenty years the Chief Sacristan of the Moravian congregation. Until the last few months of his life he was a man of perfect health, abounding spirits, and high good humor; of large frame and powerful build; "and the muscles of his brawny arms were strong as iron bands." His death, deplored by every one, resulted from a stricture of the esophagus. Three sons and two daughters, with their mother, survived him.

1903.

1204. **J. Edgar Souder.** 3, l. xvii, 7. Jan. 2. Born in Lititz, Oct. 1, 1876; a son of John and Ellen (Muecke) Souder. Married Anna M. Miller. Died of consumption.

1205. **Alberta May Pfautz.** 2, l. iii, 12. March 9. Child of Otis Pfautz.

1206. **Amos Kling.** 3, l. xvii, 8. June 28. Born in Warwick, April 19, 1863; a son of Frederick and Catharine (Herckel) Kling.

1207. **Beatus Showers.** 3, l. iii, 13 Child of Adam Showers.

1208. **Reuben Peter Grosh.** 3, l. xxii, 14. Nov. 2. A son of Timothy and Catharine Grosh, born in Lititz, Feb. 17, 1841. Married Thamar Diehm. By trade a carpenter and coach-maker.

1209. **Elvira Cora Rickert.** 2, l. xxv, 7. Nov. 12. Born in Mount Joy, March 6, 1833; a daughter of Alexander and Mary (Rathvon) Dysart. Married Ferdinand D. Rickert. She taught in the Lititz Public School for eight terms. Was a Deaconess of the Congregation.

1904.

1210. **Ada Amanda Reidenbach.** 2, l. xiii, 13. Jan. 10. Unmarried Sister. Born in Lititz, Sept. 14, 1863; a daughter of Adam B. and Fianna (Pfautz) Reidenbach. She taught in the local Public School and in the Foster Home in Philadelphia, and she was an alto singer in the church-choir. She died of pleuro-pneumonia.

1211. **Matilda Geitner.** 2, l. xiii, 12. Jan. 13. Unmarried Sister. A daughter of Jacob and Johanna (Beck) Geitner, born in Lititz, April 18, 1819. Died of pneumonia.

1212. **Peter Shaeffer Reist.** 3, l. xvii, 9. Feb. 3. A son of Jacob and Anna (Shaeffer) Reist, he was born in Warwick Township, March 7, 1823. He spent the larger part of his life as a farmer in this county and in the State of Illinois. In 1877 he retired from active life and settled in Lititz.

1213. **Mary Reidenbach.** 2, l. xxv, 8. March 19. Daughter of Jacob and Hannah (Wetzler) Burgess, born near Churchtown, Lancaster Co., on Jan. 3, 1829. Widow of John Reidenbach.

1214. **Reuben Orth Albright.** 3, l. xxi, 15. April 7. Born in Lititz, Feb. 23, 1822; a son of Gottfried and Elizabeth (Romig) Albright, and a grandson of Andrew Albright, the gunmaker. Latterly a member of the Lancaster Moravian Church. Served his country in the Civil War—195th Penna. Volunteers.

1215. **Martha Elizabeth Fass.** 2, l. iii, 11. Oct. 17. Daughter of David Fass. Died of diphtheria, aged eight years.

1216. **Mary Rebecca Zook.** 2, l. iii, 10. Dec. 18. Infant of Harry W. and Lillian (Reidenbach) Zook.

321

1905.

1217. **William Enck Groff.** 3, l. iii, 14. Feb. 18. Child of Daniel and Mabel (Enck) Groff, aged one year.

1218. **Isaac Fahnestock Bomberger.** 3, l. xvii, 10. Feb. 28. Born at Rothsville, Pa., Jan. 17, 1833; a son of Christian and Anna (Fahnestock) Bomberger. Educated in John Beck's Lititz Academy. Married Sarah Brenneman. Came to Lititz in 1861, and here engaged in various pursuits. He was the local Postmaster during President Cleveland's first administration. A paralytic stroke caused his death.

1219. **Laura Naomi Burkholder.** 2, l. xiii, 11. April 1. A daughter of Amos Burkholder, born Oct. 18, 1887.

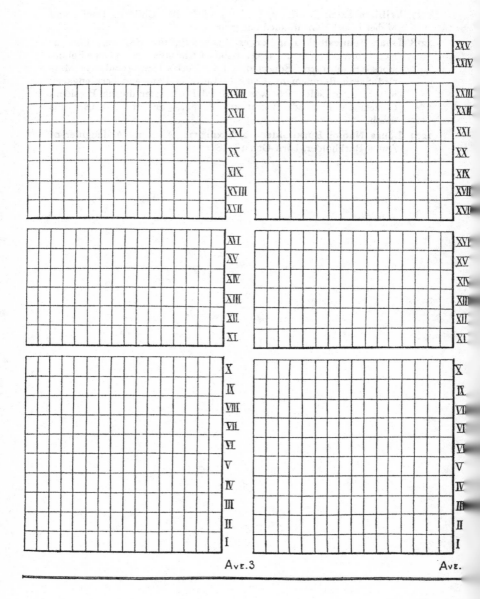

AVE.3   AVE.

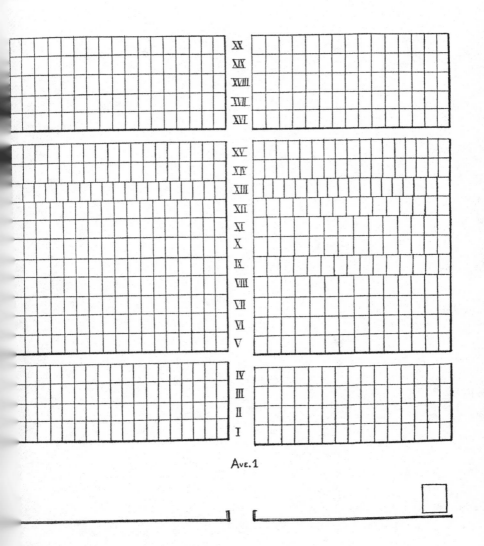

XX
XIX
XVIII
XVII
XVI
XV
XIV
XIII
XII
XI
X
IX
VIII
VII
VI
V
IV
III
II
I

Ave. 1

INDEX

TO THE

MORAVIAN GRAVEYARDS

OF

LITITZ, PENNA.

325

335

Metalmark Books is a joint imprint of The Pennsylvania State University Press and the Office of Digital Scholarly Publishing at The Pennsylvania State University Libraries. The facsimile editions published under this imprint are reproductions of out-of-print, public domain works that hold a significant place in Pennsylvania's rich literary and cultural past. Metalmark editions are primarily reproduced from the University Libraries' extensive Pennsylvania collections and in cooperation with other state libraries. These volumes are available to the public for viewing online and can be ordered as print-on-demand paperbacks.

LIBRARY OF CONGRESS CATALOGING-IN-PUBLICATION DATA

Beck, Abraham Reincke, 1833–1928.
The Moravian graveyards of Lititz, Pa., 1744–1905 / Abraham Reinke Beck.
p.   cm.
"Metalmark Books."
Summary: "A listing of burials in various Moravian cemeteries in Lititz, Pennsylvania. Originally published in 1906"—Provided by publisher.
Includes bibliographical references and index.
ISBN 978-0-271-06037-8 (pbk. : alk. paper)
1. Cemeteries—Pennsylvania—Lititz.
2. Registers of births, etc.—Pennsylvania—Lititz.
3. Moravians—Pennsylvania—Lititz—Genealogy.
4. Lititz (Pa.)—Genealogy.
I. Title.

F159.L77B43 2013
929.3748'15—dc23
2012043922

Printed in the United States of America
Reprinted by The Pennsylvania State University Press, 2012
University Park, PA 16802-1003